The Making of the Pope
2005

Recent Books by Andrew M. Greeley

SOCIOLOGY
The Catholic Myth
Religion as Poetry
The Catholic Imagination
Priests: A Calling in Crisis
The Catholic Revolution
God in the Movies (with Albert Bergesen)

FICTION
The Bishop and the Beggar Girl of St. Germain
The Bishop in the West Wing
The Bishop Goes to the University
Irish Love
Irish Stew!
Irish Cream
Second Spring
Golden Years
The Priestly Sins

The Making of the Pope 2005

Father Andrew M. Greeley

LITTLE, BROWN AND COMPANY

NEW YORK   BOSTON

Little, Brown and Company
Time Warner Book Group
1271 Avenue of the Americas, New York, NY 10020
Visit our Web site at www.twbookmark.com

First Edition: September 2005

ISBN 0-316-32560-0

LCCN 2005929908

10 9 8 7 6 5 4 3 2 1
Q-FF
Printed in the United States of America

For three who helped:

Marilyn James
June Rosner
Roberta Wilk

American Catholics love their church, but it is the church they experience every day in the priests they know and in the other Catholics in the pews with them — the church as "the people of God," not as a hierarchical institution. It is not by any means that they see these two as unrelated to each other, but they know, quite correctly, that the second is subordinate to the first and has no claim to existence except to further the first. The church is not its ruling class.

This is a distinction many Catholics could not have made before the [Second Vatican] council. Large numbers of Catholics at the time of the Reformation were in practice aware of the distinction and made it, dismayed though they were by the behavior of popes and bishops. The ecclesiology of the subsequent centuries, however, obscured this distinction badly, especially from the 19th century until the mid-20th. Critics may grieve that the teachings of Vatican II were never properly propagated, but this message about the church as a horizontal as well as a vertical reality seems to have come crashing through clear, loud and strong. Catholics may not be able to quote the council's "Dogmatic Constitution on the Church" (1964), but they got the point of that document: the church is defined in the first instance not through hierarchy and clergy, but through all its members, without regard to ecclesiastical status or office.

There are Catholics who are sincerely attached to the church, but from the church's point of view their faith is still not adequate.

John O'Malley, S.J.

I don't see how either team can win.

Warren Brown, legendary Chicago sportswriter
commenting on the 1945 World Series between
the Cubs and the Tigers

It may not matter who wins.

Blackie Ryan

Contents

∽

Dramatis Personae

Geraldo Agnelo (Brazil, 73), Archbishop of Salvador da Bahía

Francis Arinze (Nigeria, 73), Prefect of the Congregation of Divine Worship

Jorge Mario Bergoglio (Argentina, 68), Archbishop of Buenos Aires

Tarcisio Bertone (Italy, 71), Archbishop of Genoa

Godfried Danneels (Belgium, 72), Archbishop of Mechelen-Brussels

Ivan Dias (India, 69), Archbishop of Mumbai (Bombay)

Francis George (United States, 68), Archbishop of Chicago

Julián Herranz (Spain, 75), President of the Pontifical Commission for the Interpretation of Texts (Opus Dei)

Cláudio Hummes (Brazil, 71), Archbishop of São Paulo

Walter Kasper (Germany, 72), President of the Pontifical Council for Christian Unity

DRAMATIS PERSONAE

Karl Lehmann (Germany, 68), Bishop of Mainz, President of German Bishops

Theodore McCarrick (United States, 75), Archbishop of Washington

Carlo Maria Martini (Italy, 78), Emeritus Archbishop of Milan

Cormac Murphy-O'Connor (United Kingdom, 73), Archbishop of Westminster

Wilfrid Napier (South Africa, 64), Archbishop of Durban

Joaquín Navarro-Valls, Director of Vatican Press Office (Opus Dei)

Severino Polleto (Italy, 72), Archbishop of Turin

Joseph Ratzinger (Germany, 78), Prefect of the Congregation for the Doctrine of the Faith

Norberto Rivera Carrera (Mexico, 63), Archbishop of Mexico City

Oscar Andrés Rodríguez Maradiaga (Honduras, 62), Archbishop of Tegucigalpa

Christoph Schönborn (Austria, 60), Archbishop of Vienna

Angelo Scola (Italy, 64), Patriarch of Venice

Angelo Sodano (Italy, 78), Secretary of State, Vatican

Dionigi Tettamanzi (Italy, 71), Archbishop of Milan

Juan Luis Thorne (Peru, 62), Archbishop of Lima (Opus Dei)

DRAMATIS PERSONAE

John L. Allen, Vatican Correspondent, *National Catholic Reporter*

Katie Couric, Co-anchor, *Today*, NBC

Jay Levine, Chief Correspondent, Channel 2 (CBS), Chicago

Introduction

As I reread the first half of this book, I realized how angry I was. Perhaps even shrill, though I hope not. I asked myself, "Why are you so angry? You've had a good life as a priest." The Church has never oppressed me, as it does women and gays. My heterosexual celibacy has not been an overwhelming problem. I like being a priest. No one has tried to stop me from writing my columns, my novels, my sociology. There was trouble when John Cardinal Cody ruled in Chicago, but only because he dropped me beneath the radar screen and removed my name from the archdiocesan directory. Most of my fellow priests don't like me, especially because of my agitation over the sexual abuse crisis, but that was inevitable when I set my first paragraph on paper. In the spring of 2005, Tom Roberts, publisher of the *National Catholic Reporter,* asked me in Rome what price I had to pay for my work. I thought about it for a moment and said hardly any price at all.

Then why am I angry? Why was I angry in Rome? Or to put the matter more specifically, why was I angry during the 2005 conclave? Was I running for Pope? Did I have any favorite besides Cardinal Martini, who dropped out of the race, alas? No, I was angry at the whole institutional Church, of which the conclave was a manifestation. But why?

I'm angry at the Church because I love it. I began to love it when I entered St. Angela Catholic School on the West Side of Chicago in 1934, loved it when I made my first Communion in the old wooden church, loved it when I went off to the high school (day school) seminary after graduation in 1942 — the year of Stalingrad and Midway Island. I loved it when I said my first Mass in the long-awaited "new church" in 1954. I will never stop loving it. I have dedicated my fifty-one years in the priesthood to working for it. I don't regret a single day of those years. With God's help I will die in the Church and in the priesthood. As I have often said, I wonder if anyone who loves the Church can help being angry at it. It is an organized community with a divine mission made up at all levels of human beings — saints and sinners, idiots and geniuses, the devout and the indifferent, the virtuous and the corrupt, fools and brilliant thinkers, timeservers and dedicated servants, the sensitive and the clueless. It has a rich and powerfully beautiful heritage, mixed in with folk religion, superstition, ignorance, idolatry, intolerance, and hypocrisy — mountains of hypocrisy. From Peter and his bunch on down, the leadership has not been all that impressive — though it wraps itself in the aura of the sacred to disguise its stupidity, its incompetence, its dishonesty.

If the Lord had wanted a perfect Church, he would have limited its members to the angels. If he wanted dazzlingly brilliant leadership, he would have assigned those roles to the archangels. As it is, we have been led by atheists and rapists, drunkards and adulterers, child abusers and thieves, phonies and fools, traitors and liars, psychopaths and idiots.

INTRODUCTION

I've known these truths since my early years in history class at Quigley Preparatory Seminary. Why am I surprised that the Church today is less than perfect? Why be angry that our heritage of community and sacramentality is often administered by nincompoops?

I am angry because the Church has blown one of the best chances it's had in a millennium. God's Holy Spirit offered it the enormous opportunity of the Second Vatican Council, and that opportunity was blown by the shallowness of some of our clergy and religious and the loss of nerve of some of the men who made the council. I was a young priest when the council began and I was caught up in the enthusiasm of what seemed to be a new spring for the Church. The Church had suddenly become open, vibrant, and alive — far from perfect, but closer to what it ought to be and could have been for a long time if it weren't for the narrowness, fear, and timidity of its leadership.

In the more than forty years since, the Church has reversed its efforts at openness — sometimes gradually, sometimes precipitously. The trend was clear back in 1978, when I wrote about the end of Paul VI's papacy and the conclaves that elected John Paul I and, mere months later, John Paul II.

It was not merely a social scientist's curiosity nor journalistic diligence that motivated me to begin studying the "making of the Pope." When I began writing *The Making of the Popes 1978*,* I was profoundly concerned about the Church and worried about the implications of the erosion of papal credibility since 1968. John XXIII's papacy and the Second Vatican Council had occurred in my early years as a priest. My eyes were opened

---

*Andrews and McMeel, 1979.

in those days to the possibilities of a dramatic revival of the Catholic heritage, of the sort which had occurred only a few times before in history. At the same time the American Catholic Church was moving through an exciting era as it shifted from the church of the despised immigrant working class to the church of the suburban professional upper-middle class. In my first parish assignment, in the Beverly Hills district of Chicago — a magic neighborhood to begin with — I was swept up by the heady euphoria of the changes from slum to suburb and from Counter-Reformation to Ecumenical Age. I was deeply influenced by the liturgical and social action innovations permitted in the Archdiocese of Chicago by Cardinals Samuel Stritch and Albert Meyer. The latter sent me to graduate school at the University of Chicago in 1960 — just about the time that Pope John was convening the council and John Kennedy was running for president. Prospects for the Church to which I had committed my life looked bright and challenging.

Then, after 1968, it all fell apart. The hopes of the council era were spectacularly shattered as the council fathers went home and the Curia Romana, the central bureaucracy of the Church, set about the task of reestablishing its control. Disillusioned priests and nuns resigned by the thousands. Mediocrities replaced the great leaders of the council years as heads of the archdioceses in the United States.

Pope Paul VI, who succeeded John XXIII in 1963 and from whom so much had been expected, seemed somehow incapable of responding to the euphoric enthusiasm of the Catholic clergy and people. He seemed determined to reassure us that things were not moving too fast, when in fact most of us thought they were not moving fast enough.

Then, as enthusiasm declined, and frustration increased, there came on a summer day in 1968 the long-expected birth control encyclical, which rejected the Pope's own commission's recommendations for change. Like many other American Catholics, I could not believe the arbitrary sweeping away, with a wave of the papal hand, of the reasons his commission had advanced for a change in position. I told friends at Grand Beach, Michigan, my summer home, that people would not accept the encyclical and that it would be a disaster for the Church.

How many of them would not accept it and how great a disaster it would be, however, came as a shock six years later, when my colleagues at the National Opinion Research Center, William McCready and Kathleen McCourt, and I did a "before and after" study of the Second Vatican Council's impact on Catholic schools.* We had anticipated that it was the council which had led to the decline in Church practice that everyone was observing. There seemed to be little doubt in the conventional Catholic wisdom — both liberal and conservative — that the council produced the crisis American Catholicism was suffering; the only difference was over whether the problem was the council itself or the slow pace of its implementation.

But our research demonstrated that the council had been a huge success and that the decline in Church practice could be accounted for almost entirely by reactions to the birth control encyclical. The American hierarchy pooh-poohed our findings, and so did many of the Catholic Wise Persons, who referred vaguely to long-run "secularization trends." But no one found anything wrong with our mathematical models; and one archbishop who

*Catholic Schools in a Declining Church, Sheed and Ward, 1976.

had repeated the party line in public told me privately, "You're right, of course; I can't sleep often at night because of what that goddamn encyclical did in my diocese."

Unlike a lot of other clergy-scholars of my generation, I still cared about the papacy. As a sociologist I saw it as the most important religious leadership position in the world; the years of John XXIII had given a hint of what a Pope could do if he understood its world-impact potential. I also believed in the importance of leadership in any human institution; I had seen what happened to my own diocese when the religious leader lost credibility among his clergy and people. I was watching the same thing happen in the whole Church. Perhaps we'd had too much emphasis on the Pope, as a number of my European colleagues argued; perhaps another unsuccessful pontificate would be a good thing because it would complete the elimination of the "cult of personality" from the Pope's office. But I doubted it. The issue in my mind was (and is) not whether we need a Pope in Christendom but what kind we need. If we didn't have an office like that of Pope, we would have to invent it; the question is not whether we can dispense with papal leadership, but rather what style of leadership would be most effective given the circumstances of our time.

I had high hopes for Pope John Paul II. Because he was an intellectual and a poet, I assumed that he was also a liberal. He had been a liberal at the Second Vatican Council. The men who elected him (including Franz König of Vienna, who had turned the tide toward him inside the conclave) thought they were getting a liberal Pope. In fact, like Paul VI, he had lost his nerve. He tried to impose unity on the Church from the outside by stern authority. It didn't work, but his marvelously charismatic personality won him the admiration of many Catholics all over the world, who paid no attention to many of his teachings.

My beloved Church in the United States continued to fall apart for the next three decades as the quality of the hierarchy deteriorated, vocations diminished, and the laity became more independent in their religious judgments. The sexual abuse crisis, about which I had started to write in 1986, proved that we were led in many cases by incompetents and liars who deliberately covered up for the sexual pleasures of priests while trying to constrain the sexual pleasures of married laypeople.

By the end of John Paul's papacy, the institutional church in the United States was in chaos and close to collapse. As I looked around at the wreckage, I was sad and angry. Just a little bit of attention to social science (not necessarily mine) would have been an enormous help. But the leaders had the Holy Spirit; they didn't need sociology.

I thought often in Rome during the 2005 conclave that I should have left well enough alone. I shouldn't have come back twenty-seven years later to see how the cardinals (not nearly so gifted a group this time around) would cope with the crisis that they themselves had helped to create by their arrogance and ignorance (with some happy exceptions). But conclave watching was an addiction I could not resist.

I decided early on that I would not try to predict the winner this time around. My friend and colleague John L. Allen, the Rome bureau chief of the *National Catholic Reporter* — and, by dint of hard work, honesty, and heroic fairness, the best Vatican reporter of our time — was writing about the political jockeying inside the Vatican. My book, by contrast, would be a personal diary taking stock of the Church at the close of John Paul II's reign and watching the events of the weeks between funeral and conclave through the eye of a priest and professional sociologist. As it turned out, predicting the outcome and its dynamics was child's play because the Italian media provided a day-by-day account of the campaign that proceeded under transparent veils of secrecy.

It will be obvious to the reader that I am a reformer. *Ecclesia semper reformanda,* as the old dictum says — the Church always needs reform. The pace of reform is always too slow because there is always inertia in groups made up of human beings. For the Church the temptation is to postpone reform long after due season because it is a religious institution concerned with sacred matters. It has paid a heavy price through its history for the self-deceptions that have blocked changes.

However, I'm not a doctrinal reformer. I have no qualifications to speak on the development of Catholic doctrine, save to point out the many cases where it has happened. These are matters for theologians. By training, choice, and perhaps genetic disposition, I am a social scientist. I know Catholic doctrine and believe it. However, my competence is not in timeless and eternal verities, but in contingent and mutable realities; not in theoretical questions of how people should behave, but in the practical matters of how they do behave; not in the ultimate truths of the Catholic faith, but in the structural realities of the institution's attempt to teach these truths. If a reader wants to know what I believe or what I preach, my spiritual diaries are available in bookstores and my homilies for the past ten years are on my Web page (www.agreeley.com). But these are not the perspectives that shape this book.

When I tell Church leaders that they have suffered a catastrophic loss of credibility on sexual and reproductive issues even among the clergy, I am not arguing that they should change their teaching. Rather I am suggesting that instead of blaming secularism or materialism or relativism (or whatever other "isms" they may list) for this decline in credibility, they should ask whether they themselves may have failed to understand the problems of their laity and failed also to teach them and preach to them in terms they might understand. Blaming someone else or abstract historical trends is a poor excuse for not examining one's own failures to teach and preach effectively — activities that necessarily involve ongoing communication with their people. To teach and preach one must first of all listen.

Thus on some of the hot-button Catholic issues that dominate the American media, I am agnostic. I am skeptical of the assumption that if the Church would ordain women priests and permit priests to marry all would be well. The evidence that my colleague Mark Chaves of the University of Arizona adduced in his book on women clergy demonstrates pretty clearly that the presence of women in the clergy does not appreciably enhance the status of women in a denomination.* My own work (in *Priests: A Calling in Crisis*†) suggests that celibate Catholic clergy are happier both personally and professionally than married Protestant clergy. I suspect from anecdotal evidence that the same finding would emerge in research comparing Latin Rite Catholic celibates with married Byzantine Rite Catholic or Greek Orthodox clergy. If the Vatican should authorize a married priesthood next week, the communication problems would persist between a highly centralized Church leadership and a

*Ordaining Women: Culture and Conflict in Religious Organizations, Harvard University Press, 1999.
†University of Chicago Press, 2004.

global laity of a billion people, a large proportion of whom have college educations. The reforms in which I am interested would deal with the problems inherent in this situation.

If asked, "What about birth control? Shouldn't the Church change that teaching?" I have to plead agnosticism. Others must decide the answer to that question. However, I can reply that in the countries on which we have data, approximately nine out of ten Catholics do not believe that birth control is seriously wrong. That doesn't mean the Church should change its teaching. It means rather that it has an enormous credibility problem on this issue, and that the leadership must ask why the old pedagogical method of saying, in effect, "This is a rule you must keep," doesn't work anymore. When I say this to a Church leader, I usually face a glazed expression which suggests that the person does not really comprehend what empirical observation based on solid evidence means. Hence, he is certainly not ready for my suggested explanation: "Maybe you folks didn't do a very good job of teaching and preaching because you haven't done a good job of listening."

The breakdown in communication is evident at the very lowest level of the institutional Church, the local parish. In *Priests: A Calling in Crisis* I speculated that the rectory doors must be made of steel to prevent the clergy from hearing the words of their parishioners. Only 2 percent of the priests thought quality of preaching was a serious spiritual problem for the laity, while 80 percent of the laity thought so. This kind of problem, I suggest, extends all the way up to the fifth floor of the Vatican Palace.

No one listens.

No one knows what's going on.

Pope John Paul said in his Exhortation on Marriage and the Family that the experience of the married laity was an indispensable source for the Church to understand sexuality. However, practically no one — from the local rectory to the Vatican — is listening to the sexual experience of the married laity.

I began my three-decades-long study of conclaves with little hope that my perspective on these issues would be taken seriously. The fathers of the Vatican Council, while not anticipating the destabilization their changes would introduce into the Church, nonetheless introduced mechanisms to cope with change — the theory of collegiality and the institution of the Synod of Bishops (which Paul VI, with characteristic nervous caution, had watered down). Yet since the end of the council there has been very little collegiality at any level in the Church, and the Synod of Bishops, it is generally agreed, has become a waste of time.

I doubt that the leadership of the Church will hear what I'm saying about structural reform. Priests complained about my findings on parishioners' reaction to sermons by arguing that since I did not do full-time parish work, I did not know what was happening in parishes. I responded, in vain, that I had data on what parishioners think based on a valid national sample — and perhaps they didn't know what their own parishioners think. At every level in the Church — up to the Vatican Palace — no one wants to hear a Cassandra who calls for complete reversal not of doctrine but of governance style and structure. No one wants to hear that the only way out of the present Big Muddy is not less change but more, change not in doctrinal matters but in the fundamental assumptions of clerical culture.

Theologians (or the theologically trained, which would include many if not most priests) and sociologists see the world very differently. Theologians see it in sharp colors and describe it in sweeping (and often self-serving) generalizations. Sociologists see it in many shades of gray and describe it in problematic, qualified, and partial assertions. Theologians would say, for example, the people in their parish are lacking in faith. Sociologists would say that some have very strong faith and others do not and many are somewhere in between, perhaps more in the first category than there would have been fifty years ago.

Theologians would assert that Western Europe has become secularized and pagan. Sociologists would respond that there has been an increase in belief in life after death (a faith in transcendence, at least) among cohorts born since 1945 — and that those who think Europe was once seriously Christian are not familiar with the recent literature on the social history of Europe.

Sociologists might conclude the argument with the comment that theologists are doing sociology too and on the cheap. They are describing the modern world without any serious investigation and in the absence of data. They are in fact reducing the blooming, buzzing pluralism of human life to reified abstract concepts — like consumerism or relativism or secularism.

The argument cannot be settled in this book, nor perhaps ever. In the years I shared editorial board responsibilities with a group of European theologians (mostly German), I learned that a "positivist" — which was how they labeled me — can never prevail in an argument with Platonist theologians because they know everything.

However, this sketch of the argument — critical, I think, for understanding the contemporary Church — will at least demonstrate to the reader that my story of the current situation in the Church and of the 2005 conclave comes from a perspective that is, if not unique, different from most other such stories. *Caveat lector.*

INTRODUCTION

Priests tell me that I am angry because the bishops haven't listened to me. Not that they haven't listened to me personally, but that they don't listen to any of us who try to study society and social institutions systematically. They reject the bad news — the people, they say, are finally accepting the birth control teaching. But they also reject the good news: religion is not dead in Europe; priests are the happiest men in America, happier even than married Protestant ministers; the Catholic schools make an essential contribution to the American Church.

Before the fact, I would have considered the election of Cardinal Joseph Ratzinger as an extension of the papacy's inwardness and authoritarianism, with perhaps more Teutonic efficiency and German theological abstraction.

When I heard he had selected the name Benedict, however, I suspended judgment. This nod to a Pope who specialized in healing offered reason for hope. Perhaps here was a surprise trump card of the Spirit.

Perhaps not.

In any case I stand by three conclusions I drew from my time in Rome: that the conclave must be expanded and become not only more apparently democratic but actually democratic; that the time for secret elections of the leader of a billion people has long since ended; and that the current goals of the Church, especially the reevangelization of Western Europe, will require that Church leaders learn to listen.

Moreover, despite my weariness and discouragement, my frustration and near despair, I left Rome reassured that the Church is still very much alive.

Andrew M. Greeley
May 2005

PART I

Chicago, October 15, 2003

There is much festivity in Rome these days. October brings the twenty-fifth anniversary of John Paul II, the beatification of Mother Teresa, and a consistory for the creation of thirty-one new cardinals. There's a lot of coverage in the American media — an apotheosis of the Pope, but also a display of his frailty. Frank Bruni does a piece in the *New York Times* about the handful of men who are running the Church because of John Paul's weakness. The Pope will not resign, even if he has to take to his bed. He believes that a father does not resign from his family.

With the media spotlight on our eighty-three-year-old Pope, Catholicism is celebrated but also made to look a little ridiculous. I have gut instincts against the personality cult that has grown up around John Paul, but he is entitled to a celebration. He has been an impressive influence for the last quarter century.

How does one evaluate his administration? In my book on the conclaves of 1978, I was ecstatic about him. I thought that he would carry the reforms of the Second Vatican Council on to their logical conclusion — a more democratic, sensitive, open Church. I admit that I was terribly wrong.

He surely is one of the most talented men ever to be Pope, an actor, a poet, a philosopher, a man of enormous personal charm. He has had a tremendous impact on the Catholic Church and on

3

the world. *Time* magazine rates him one of the "men of the century." Some authors (like Jonathan Kwitny in his book *Man of the Century**) argue that he brought down the socialist empire of the Soviet Union. He has traveled abroad tirelessly. Everywhere he has been hailed by massive crowds of enthusiastic Catholics. He has involved himself in the politics of countries like Nigeria and Cuba as well as his native Poland. He has lectured world leaders, including President Clinton. He has put his stamp irrevocably on the Catholic Church. He has, according to many, restored order and discipline to a Church which was in chaos during the years after the Second Vatican Council. Still others would say he has saved the Church from the folly of Pope John XXIII.

He sincerely believes that he is loyal to the Second Vatican Council, in which he participated. Yet he has virtually ignored the principle of collegial consultation with the bishops which that council endorsed, most notably in his unilateral declaration that women cannot become priests. Bishops are once again treated like lower-level bureaucrats who are servants of the Roman Curia. Their triennial synods in Rome are manipulated by the Curia.

He has hassled theologians and scholars at the cost of diminishing the freedom of discussion that the council seemed to support. He has appointed extremely conservative bishops. He has sternly lectured married laypeople about the immorality of birth control. He has brought ecumenical discussions virtually to a halt. Although he was one of the principal architects of the conciliar document on the Church and the modern world, he seems profoundly suspicious of the modern world. He refuses to consider the ordination of married men and makes it difficult and

*Henry Holt and Company, 1997.

humiliating for men who wish to leave the priesthood to marry. He has encouraged right-wing organizations like Opus Dei and the Legionnaires of Christ, which have in effect become diligent hunters of heresy.

All of these actions have led many to speak of him as a Pope of "restoration," a Pope who has restored to his office and to the Vatican the power and the attitudes of Pope Pius XII (1939–58).

On social and political issues, however, his orientation could hardly be called conservative. He condemns war and the death penalty, defends the rights of immigrants, and denounces anti-Semitism — all of which make him far more "liberal" than most Catholics.

There isn't much debate that he has been intent on the restoration of order, discipline, and obedience to the Church. If one believes that such a restoration is good, then one indeed thinks he is the Pope of the Century. If one believes that such restoration is mistaken, unnecessary, and counterproductive, then one has profound reservations about his papacy.

I don't doubt his greatness. I wish that he had been more collaborative in his governance and less authoritarian in his style. I wish his many global visits (over a hundred now) had been fact-finding instead of manifestations. I wish above all he had not aborted the reform in the Church. I even wish he had pushed ahead with a reform of the papacy itself.

However, no one is perfect. I can disagree with him, respectfully, and still admire him.

The new cardinals don't impress. Justin Rigali, a former curialist and destined to move from St. Louis to Philadelphia, gets the red hat, and Michael Fitzgerald, the specialist on Islam who heads the Interreligious Dialogue office, does not. A lot of unfamiliar third-world names. There is talk now that there will certainly be a third-world Pope. That doesn't make me enthusiastic, because third-world bishops tend to be more Roman than the Romans. I'm glad I scheduled my upcoming reconnaissance to Rome when things calm down a little.

ROME, NOVEMBER 9, 2003

This place is weird.

You used to be able to walk into St. Peter's and say a prayer. Not anymore. They have made part of the plaza a kind of amphitheater for papal performances. You can get in only through the north entrance, and you must go through metal screeners, a sign of the time, I guess. There are nine screeners, but only one seems to be operating. The queue stretches all the way around the colonnade and back to the Via Conciliazione. Given the notorious inefficiency and indifference of the Italian police, the screening is probably pro forma. St. Peter's certainly would be an ideal target for terrorism, particularly at the time of a papal election. Still, in earlier times you could walk into San Pietro and say a prayer to the Lord whenever you wanted, just like back home. Except back home now the clergy keep the churches locked all day, so that the laity can't make the once popular "visits to the Blessed Sacrament." Here you can, if you're willing to stand in line for an hour.

A metal fence has been built around the obelisk that Pope Sixtus put in the middle of the Piazza. Some of my best photos of the last conclaves were of the *ragazzi* (boy punks) climbing all over the base. They can't do it anymore, which seems like a notable loss. Huge construction edifices have been erected in front of the press office on one side of the Conciliazione and the Congregation for Bishops on the other side, thus effectively blocking much of the view of the church as you walk up the street. Worse still, the edifices have been turned into billboards. There doesn't seem to be any construction going on, so the locals claim that the whole purpose is to earn billboard income!

I don't think I believe that, but it does add to the weirdness of the situation. The Pope is sick, probably terminally. People say that Cardinal Sodano, secretary of state, and Archbishop Dziwisz, the Pope's personal secretary (often called Don Stanislaus), are running the Church, sometimes with disagreements between them. The present quasi interregnum may be long.

Even weirder, it seems to me, is the absence of conversation about a successor. There was so much discussion in past years about the Pope's health and a conclave that speculation seems to have run out of steam. More seriously, perhaps, the Sacred College seems less distinguished than it has been in a long time, a subject to which I will return later. Thus the Vatican is a strange, gray, almost depressed place. My friend Adolfo says maybe an old man recalls excitement of earlier years that didn't really exist. I don't believe it for a minute. The celebration to mark the Pope's twenty-fifth anniversary on the Throne of the Fisherman (who in his most fantastical moments could not have imagined having a throne) was a bright, almost gaudy event. When it was over, however, the weariness returned, not merely of the Pope but also of the Vatican and of the Church. Despite his successes John Paul will leave the Catholic Church with serious problems of governance, including a somewhat listless Sacred College and an undistinguished episcopate. I will reflect on that later when I've had more chance to talk to people.

I lunched today with John Allen of the *National Catholic Reporter*, and a monsignor who is in charge of the permission for the Tridentine Latin Mass came into the restaurant. (If some want to reinstitute the Tridentine Mass, it's all right with me, so long as they don't try to impose it on the rest of us — which of course is their goal.) This man refuses to say the Mass of Paul VI — the modern Mass — around the edges of which the current reactionaries at the Congregation for Divine Worship are eating away. He also believes that the Pope is a heretic: strong on "morals" (meaning sex), John Paul is weak on faith. Hence, for example, his prayers with various kinds of heretics, schismatics, and infidels at the Assisi interreligious dialogues these past several years. The Pope is a philosopher, the priest says, but unfortunately not a theologian — a criticism one also hears from liberal theologians!

There is one aspect of John Paul's administrative style about which most people are unaware. While he signs almost every document the curialists bring him, he pays rather little attention to what they are doing. Many of them have been consistently upset at the Pope because he would rather roam around the world than stay at home and tend to business — by which they mean their business.

The Curia is composed of the Secretariat of State (a "prime minister"); nine Congregations (for example, Doctrine of the Faith, Divine Worship, Making of Bishops); three Tribunals; eleven Pontifical Councils (Christian Unity, Family, Interreligious Dialogue, Social Communications); five Offices (Economic Affairs); and eleven commissions or committees (Historical Sciences, Bible). Its members do not necessarily share a common ideology, save for maintaining their own power, as does every bureaucracy.

Popes for the last half century have dealt with the entrenched power and age-old culture of the Curia (or one should say powers, since there are many internal divisions within the Curia) in many different ways. Pius XII ran the Church though his housekeeper, Madre Pasqualina (who actually accompanied him into the conclave at which he was elected Pope). John XXIII used the Vatican Council as a counterweight to curial imperatives. John Paul II signs their documents and ignores them. One would think that someday a Pope might simply abolish the Curia and create a more modern civil service.

So as I say, this is a weird city, sometimes tragic, sometimes comic, sometimes both. Yet as I watch the faithful of every hue under heaven walk to and fro in front of the great basilica (which started the Reformation and cost us Germany), I am impressed once again by the majesty of the building and the enormous strength of the Catholic imagination, which binds us all together.

ROME, NOVEMBER 10, 2003

I reflect tonight that the Catholic Church is in deep trouble. It is fractured, polarized. The right is small in numbers but because of its influence on the present Pope large in power. The left is increasingly alienated. The center leans sharply to the left on matters of sexuality. Few Catholics, even the "good" ones, listen to the Vatican or take it seriously.

Those who want the cork back in the bottle will be happy with the papacy of John Paul II. Those who do not will be unhappy, regardless of *Time* magazine's judgments. There remains also a pragmatic question of whether his restoration has been effective. Have order and discipline been restored in the Church or have the laity and the lower clergy simply gone their own way, cheered for the Pope when he has come to their country, but made their own decisions? Has the persecution of some theologians stopped other theologians from speculations that go much further than those of comparatively moderate men like Hans Kung? Are the conservative bishops he has appointed able to turn the tide against those who believe in and want greater cultural and theological pluralism, more lay participation, less hierarchy, more dialogue?

This is an empirical question that is not answered by the ecstatic enthusiasms of conservative Catholics or by the praise of bishops. Has the restoration worked? If it hasn't, might there have been other and more subtle and sophisticated methods for tempering the explosive enthusiasms generated by the Vatican Council and Pope John? One does not arrive at doctrines by taking surveys. But one can measure with survey data whether a policy perspective enforced for two decades has been successful. Catholic conservatives will perhaps insist that it is not necessary that a Pope's policy be successful, but merely that he lay down the law and demand that people obey him. Yet this is a narrow and rigid view of the role of a teacher. At this period in the history of the human species — and perhaps at any period — the good teacher must persuade, no matter how lofty his position. Whether the Pope should persuade or not may be debatable. One can nonetheless ask whether he has persuaded on those matters he considers most important.

I will take as criteria three positions which it is not unfair to say the Pope has made central to his policy of restoration — abortion, birth control, and married priests. Each position has a different theological valence. Abortion has traditionally been considered a moral evil whose rejection is central to Catholic morality. Birth control has been forbidden, but no one claims by infallible authority. Clerical celibacy is a disciplinary matter that could be changed tomorrow.

In many different countries on which data are available — the United States, the United Kingdom, Spain, the Federal Republic, Italy, the Netherlands, France, Belgium, Ireland, Canada, Austria, even Poland — any changes that have occurred in the last twenty years have been counter to the Pope's aims. In all those countries but Poland the majority also favor the ordination of women. Moreover, on such issues as birth control, masturbation, and in vitro fertilization, for example, the lower clergy are clearly on the side of the laity. The restoration has not worked.*

Some might argue that I ought not to evaluate the success or failure of a papal administration. That's God's job. Yet historians have evaluated the success or failure of papal tenures for at least half a millennium. No leader in the world, dead or alive, is so exalted that he is above criticism.

The Pope has lectured laypeople that birth control is wrong because it interferes with the complete gift of spouses to one another. It is not an argument that most married laypeople are inclined to take seriously. Indeed, many dismiss it — if they even hear it — as what one would expect from a celibate who has no

*See the data in my books *The Catholic Imagination* and *The Catholic Revolution,* University of California Press, 2001, 2004.

sense of how essential sexual love is to heal the frictions and the hurts of the common life. For all the enthusiasm that meets the papal visitor when his plane touches down, the harsh truth is that the papacy has lost all credibility on human sexuality. Indeed, there are very few issues that affect modern life — the death penalty, war, and immigration, for example — on which the laity listen to what the Pope says. If John Paul II intended his restoration to reestablish the credibility of the papacy, it seems to have had the opposite effect. The next Pope will face the situation of a Catholic population that cheers but does not listen. With the exception of the Netherlands, there has not been a massive withdrawal of Catholics from their religion,* but there has been a withdrawal of credibility from Church authority, even more among Catholic women than among Catholic men.

One need merely pick up an issue of a theological journal or attend a meeting of theologians to realize that order and discipline have not been preserved. Or listen to a conversation of priests to understand that in the absence of any credible authority, most deal with pastoral problems (such as homosexuality) by following their own instincts and not the dictates of the steady stream of Roman documents.

Moreover, it is clear from research in several countries that the Catholic laity favor a more democratic Church structure — one in which the Pope has representative lay advisers, local priests and laity elect their own bishops, the national conferences of bishops have more independence, and there is more concern for the religious problems of the laity than for major

---

*See my book *Religion in Europe at the End of the Second Millennium,* Transaction Publishing, 2002.

theological issues. Virtually no one leaves the Church over these issues, but they are attitudes that Church leadership can hardly ignore if it wishes to regain its credibility. None of the changes that the laity desire would affect the essence of Catholicism in the slightest, and some would represent a return to more traditional Catholic practices, such as the election of a bishop by priests and people. They are all, however, utterly foreign to Pope John Paul's perspective on the role of Church authority. For weal or woe, absolute obedience is, for most people, a thing of the past. If one permits one's laity to obtain an education, then one must learn to listen to them and try to persuade them.

Nor are Americans the most radical of Catholics in their longing for a more democratically organized Church. The Spaniards and the Irish are even more "radical," as measured by numbers supporting change in the Church's organization. Perhaps if your own democratic societies work very well, you wonder why your Church can't adopt the same governmental style. At the least, you wonder why they can't listen to you once in a while.

It is unlikely that the Pope would be troubled by evidence that his restoration has not been successful. He firmly believes, it would seem, that it is his mission to lead the Church back to the path of fidelity. Did not Our Lady of Fatima turn away the hand of the Turkish gunman to prevent his death? With that kind of self-perception, one is not inclined to question one's instincts about the kind of leadership the Church needs.

Some Catholic conservatives (who are no more than 5 percent of Catholics in the Western European and North Atlantic countries) lament that the Pope hasn't been tough enough in his restoration. He should excommunicate Catholic married people who practice birth control and theologians who dare to question his teachings. Only that stern discipline will effectively restore the Church to what it was before the disaster of the Second Vatican Council. It is clear by now, however, that the Pope has no taste for such measures, that he is too kindly and gentle a man to engage in hardball tactics. He still seems to believe that if he demands obedience often enough and strongly enough and in enough countries, eventually he will obtain it.

Curiously the "liberal" cardinals who presided over the Second Vatican Council voted for Cardinal Wojtyla because they considered him one of their own. They expected a continuation of the spirit of the Second Vatican Council as they understood it. Franz König of Vienna — one of the most articulate leaders of the procouncil party — in violation of the strict rules of the conclave, spoke up to urge his colleagues to vote for the cardinal archbishop of Kraców. The curial reactionaries voted to the bitter end for their anticouncil favorite, Cardinal Siri of Genoa.

When König resigned at the age of seventy-five, the Pope appointed a new archbishop of Vienna without consulting König or anyone else. It would seem that the basis for this appointment was an encounter between the Pope and Father Hans Hermann Groer, a Benedictine abbot, at a Marian conference. The Pope was deeply impressed with the abbot's devotion to the Mother of Jesus. Under such circumstances no other consultation was necessary — even if the man was as different from Cardinal König as anyone could be.

If there had been consultation, the Pope would perhaps have learned that there were charges of pedophilia against the abbot. When these charges became public, they created an enormous scandal in Austria. Rome, however, chose not to intervene after it accepted Cardinal Groer's resignation (submitted because of age before the pedophile charges surfaced). Finally his successor, Cardinal Schönborn, had to issue a statement (together with three other Austrian bishops) saying that the charge was substantially true. Groer was forced to promise that he would never act as bishop or cardinal again and would go into exile. His parting words were hardly an admission of guilt or an apology. So Schönborn apologized for him. The Vatican's denial and stonewalling, not unlike that practiced by the American bishops, turned into a disaster, one that the Vatican has yet to put behind it and probably never will.

Cardinal König, now in his nineties,* is still popular with Austrian Catholics. If the Pope had chosen to consult with him about his successor, this story would have been very different.

Perhaps John Paul's tragic flaw was his refusal to consult, much less to govern collaboratively. Just as in Vienna he deprived himself of the insights of a man who knew the local situation far better than he did, so too by his refusal to consult other bishops and the Catholic laity, he cut himself off from crucial information. He himself has written that married laypeople can offer an indispensable contribution to the Church's understanding of marriage. But only laity who already agree with the Pope are ever chosen for consultation.

I do not question the Pope's piety or intelligence or sincerity. I question only the wisdom of his policy. Many other Popes have made mistakes. I believe that for all his talent he has made a serious mistake by not listening. Surely there was some chaos in the years after the Second Vatican Council, especially among the clergy — though not as much as the Pope and some of his advisers

*He died after this diary entry.

think. Most Catholic laity are not at all confused. Complaints about the confusion of the laity come from (usually) wealthy conservative Catholics who are opposed to the Second Vatican Council and from hierarchs who project onto the laity unease of their own.

Can there be reform without some chaos? Did the chaos require a frontal, authoritarian attack? The evidence suggests that it did not.

One hears it said often — especially in Rome, but among conservative Catholics everywhere — that the prestige of the Catholic Church is at an all-time high. But is it really? Does it have more prestige today than when John XXIII was alive and hope was strong among both laity and clergy, when the brisk winds of change were blowing through the Church? When the Second Vatican Council was leaving behind century-old encrustation and facing the modern world with bravery and confidence, with a hopeful heart and an open mind? In Rome one hears it said these days that Pope John was a silly old man. Was he really? Or was his direction the best one for the Church? Either he or John Paul was mistaken in his policy decisions. Which one was it? For all the prestige the Pope has acquired for the Church, is it really more attractive to its own members and to others today than it was in the time of Pope John? Or is the prestige hollow, granted to a very gifted man and not to an institution that is stagnating once again?

The Church today has fewer bright lights than at any time since the end of the Second World War. The College of Cardinals has some good men, but lacks, for the most part, distinguished men of the sort Pius XII appointed (and who shaped the Vatican Council) and those whom Pope John himself appointed.

There are no giants like Lienart of Lille, Frings of Cologne, Alfrink of the Netherlands, Suenens of Malines, König of Vienna, Lacaro of Bologna, Etchegaray of Marseilles, Meyer of Chicago, Ritter of St. Louis, Arns of São Paulo, Lorscheider of Fortaleza, Tarancon of Seville. Indeed, one would have to look carefully at the present list to find more than a handful of standouts.

Some bishops are impressive, but they are almost accidental, the result of someone's mistake. The Sacred College and the world episcopate are gray, meek, and mediocre. The thinkers and the doers are not wanted because there is a suspicion that they are not doctrinally orthodox and not sufficiently docile. They are the kind of men who might not be content to be invisible in the light of the papal sun.

The Curia, as always, is caught up in its own culture of infighting (thus the Congregation for Divine Worship effectively condemns, in its documents, events that happen at the papal masses). The Secretariat of State is in frequent conflict with the Congregation for the Doctrine of the Faith (formerly called the Holy Office of the Inquisition). The Curia attracts few bright lights and it quickly extinguishes those who by some mischance drift into it. Many able men refuse to serve in it because they perceive it as a kind of death sentence.

The staffs of the pontifical universities suffer the same problem. Many good scholars do not want to live and work in Rome, where they are always in the spotlight of suspicion. Catholic theology around the world, so creative and exciting (and orthodox) after the war, is in a kind of lethargy created in part by Roman suspicion. There are no men of the caliber or influence of the postwar theologians like Karl Rahner, Yves Congar, John Courtney Murray, Hans Kung, and the younger Joseph Ratzinger.

Finally, the people to whom I've spoken in Rome insist that young men coming into the priesthood these days rarely show the kind of intelligence and vigor that one would want in ecclesiastical leadership. What chance is there that the fractures in the Church will be healed by uninspired leaders?

In short, the Church of Pius XII produced great leaders and thinkers in abundance, and the Church in the years since the Vatican Council has not been able to match them. There are many possible explanations for this phenomenon — an emotional exhaustion after the exertions of the council, for example.

But the most important explanation is that the top leadership of the Church after Pope John has been fearful of talented individuals. There was some chaos and confusion in the immediate postcounciliar years — though not nearly as much as many ecclesiastics here in Rome believe. In its efforts to calm the Church down, the Vatican has avoided strong leaders and insightful thinkers. It much prefers men (and women) who will certainly not make trouble — and who can be counted on generally not to have many thoughts of their own. It also engages in little collaborative effort at any level because it distrusts even those whom it has appointed to important positions. In the present troubled time, the Vatican's position seems to be that only the center can be trusted to do and think the right things. No one else is needed. God's Spirit works in the Vatican and nowhere else.

Hence the light at the next conclave is likely to be pretty dim.

Rome, November 11, 2003

I met today with Phoebe Natanson of ABC and consumed a dangerously thick hot chocolate at the coffee shop near her headquarters in the Piazza Grazioli. At least I know who's in charge here for the network, though as she explained to me and as I should have remembered, networks operate in confusion and chaos when any story breaks. I will not know until the moment of the Pope's death what they want me to do, where I'm supposed to go, and what's going to happen. At least I have a phone number and a name and a friendly face.*

Someday, nonetheless, a cardinal will emerge on the balcony of San Pietro and announce that he has the name of the new Pope. Great theater indeed. We're good at that sort of thing. Not a good way to select the leader of 1.2 billion Catholics, but just now the only way we have.

The election of the head of the Catholic Church is unquestionably the oldest and the longest-functioning election on the planet. It has gone through many changes and developments since the time of Peter the Fisherman. It has, however, always been a political process, sometimes corrupt, and always pregnant with drama and fascination. One dimension of it has not changed. The Pope is elected by the clergy of Rome, as all bishops in the early days of the Catholic Church were selected by the clergy and laity of their own dioceses. The current legal fiction is that each of the cardinals is a parish priest of Rome with a parish church under his care. In fact, each parish is run by a vicar, and

---

*In fact, they wouldn't need me at all. The agreement I had to be a chief correspondent with Chris Wallace vanished when he moved to Fox.

the cardinal's responsibilities are an occasional visit and perhaps a financial contribution. Nonetheless, the custom keeps alive the tradition that a diocese should select its own leader — "He who presides over all should be chosen by all," as Pope Leo I wrote. The cardinals' role as sole electors, however, was definitively established only in the eleventh century.

The first several papal elections (the winning candidates of which were almost certainly married men) may have been to select the chairman of the ruling collegium, since at that time Rome, according to some scholars, was governed by committee and not by a monarchical bishop.

The custom of appointing cardinals who were not in fact parish priests of Rome or its suburbs began only in the thirteenth century. For most of the first thousand years of the papacy, the laity of Rome and especially their political and civic leaders played an important role in ratifying the papal election — as did the emperors: first Byzantine, then German. (Indeed, in 1903 the Austrian emperor vetoed the election of a cardinal, albeit before the fact of his election.) At times in the early Middle Ages, the Cardinals (and other clergy) would select a Pope and then bring him out on the balcony. If the people cheered, he was crowned. If they booed, the electors tried again.

In the tenth century important Roman families had de facto control of the outcome of the elections through a skilled combination of sex, bribery, and force. The most notorious of these families was the Theophylacts, whose legendary matron, Marozia, appointed and then deposed Pope John X, then appointed Pope Leo VI, then Stephen VII. She was the mistress of Pope Sergius III, whom she also appointed Pope, and after his death, she deputed their son as John XI, a young man not out of his teens. This was not a good time to be Pope. A third of Popes elected between 872 and 1012 died violent deaths, often because they resisted the schemes of the Roman nobility.

There have been repeated attempts at reform, some more successful than others. In 1059 Nicholas II decreed that the Popes should be elected by only the six cardinal bishops of the suburban sees. Several centuries after the German emperors cleaned up the mess in tenth-century Rome, Aeneas Sylvius Piccolomini (elected Pius II in 1458), left an account of the buying and selling of the papacy, which had become routine. According to Piccolomini, a Renaissance humanist, some of the (eleven) cardinals made deals in the latrines to block his election. Perhaps the most corrupt of all the elections was in 1492, when Rodrigo Borgia became Alexander VI in a conclave in which it was said that only five of the twenty-two cardinals could not be bought.

Gradually the present form of the conclave (from the Latin word for key, because the cardinals were under "lock and key") emerged. In 1179 Alexander III ruled that the winning candidate must receive two-thirds of the vote. Pius XII in 1945 added the requirement of two-thirds plus one (so that a man could not guarantee his own election). John Paul II revoked the requirement for the extra vote and decreed that after thirty-three ballots a Pope might be elected by a simple majority (a change of an eight-hundred-year-old custom which, according to some, was a way to insure that his conservative policies survived his death). Alexander III also excluded all but the three orders of cardinals (bishops, deacons, and priests) from voting, thus ending lay participation.

At the second Council of Lyons (1274) it was decreed that the electors should be locked up in a secure place, that they should sleep in a communal dormitory, and that their food supplies should be cut in half after three days if they had not elected a Pope. After five more days they were to receive only bread, wine, and water. In 1345 Clement VI permitted a curtain or a wall between beds. Only at the end of the nineteenth century did Leo XIII permit each cardinal to have his own room.

In 1505 Pope Julius II decreed that "simoniacal" elections were invalid and that anyone chosen in an election that had been bought should be considered an apostate. His own election, however, was simoniacal. Pope Pius XII, in 1945, revoked the apostasy label, and Pope Paul VI, to preserve the validity of a papal election, revoked the invalidity of such an election. Since the end of the Papal States, however, there is perhaps less grounds to worry about anyone wanting to buy an election.

The requirement of secrecy during and after the conclave was treated lightly until the last century. In the nineteenth century, the cardinal electors, often living in the Lateran Palace, walked down the street to St. John Lateran's Cathedral, where they would vote, happily chatting with the crowds that lined their path. Only with the veto of the candidacy of Cardinal Rampola by the Austrian emperor Franz Josef in 1903 did the rules against campaigning before the conclave and talking about it afterward become strict. Pope Paul VI and Pope John Paul II made these violations punishable by the most solemn of excommunications. Nonetheless, campaigning goes on while a Pope is still alive and more overtly after his death — though now it is called "consulting." Moreover, the pattern of voting and indeed the votes of each elector are eventually known, sometimes immediately after an election. Not every cardinal elector, especially if he is Italian, takes the secrecy requirement seriously.

During the twentieth century, the cardinal electors were locked in extremely uncomfortable quarters in the Sistine Chapel, but John Paul II ordered that henceforth the electors would live in the new, hotellike St. Martha's House at the other side of the Vatican City and vote in the Sistine Chapel. Whether this arrangement will lead to further leaks while the conclave is in process remains to be seen. Pope John Paul's rules also require a careful screening of the Sistine for bugs, but there is no assurance that such precautions can outwit modern electronic eavesdropping. It is alleged that at the election in 1958, Francis Cardinal Spellman of New York sent a message from inside the chapel to the CIA resident in Rome.

Pius XII eliminated the provision for a "servant" or "valet" or "secretary" to accompany the cardinals into the conclave, though at his election in 1939, he was accompanied by his housekeeper, Madre Pasqualina, later called La Papessa. While this fact was a secret at the time and for many years thereafter, she was the first woman (that we know of) who was permitted inside a conclave.

The cardinals may go into conclave fifteen days after the death of the Pope and must begin after twenty days. They enter late in the afternoon and begin voting the next morning, after having taken the most solemn oaths of both secrecy and responsibility under Michelangelo's fresco of the Last Judgment. There are two "scrutinies" each day, one in the morning and one in the afternoon, and two ballots in each scrutiny. Each cardinal writes on a ballot the name of his candidate and deposits it in a chalice on the chapel's altar. Three cardinals count the ballots. If no one is elected, the ballots together with straw are burned in a stove with a chimney that reaches to the roof of the chapel. Black smoke appears from the chimney and those outside mutter in disgust, "E nero." However, if someone is elected, the straw is omitted and (sometimes) a tiny trickle of white smoke appears to exultant shouts of "E bianco!" (In the two elections of 1978 the Vatican had a hard time producing white smoke.) Shortly thereafter, the senior cardinal deacon appears with full solemnity on the balcony of St. Peter's and announces, for example, "I have joyous news for you!" (Cheers.) "We have a Pope!" (More cheers.) "Charles Cardinal of the Holy Roman Church Wojtyla!" (Yet more cheers.) "Who chooses for himself the name of John Paul!" (Most cheers of all.)

Inside the most recent conclaves some men have been called Great Electors: the men who have influence, power, intelligence, and a clear notion of what they want for the Church (such as Leo Suenens in the 1965 conclave and Franz König in the second 1978 conclave, both to their later regret). Others, perhaps not so gifted, are content to follow along with the dynamics of the voting, which dynamics they attribute (rather at odds with traditional Catholic teaching) to the influence of the Holy Spirit (and thus deny that the conclave is a human political event). It is most important to an elector to be able to go home and claim that he voted for the winner even before the winner was clear.

Who will it be this time? My favorite would be Cardinal Danneels of Mechelen-Brussels, a bright light of intelligence and sensitivity, a man who knows what's going on. However, he is thought to be too liberal and has had a heart attack. He does not bother to hide what he thinks, which is a dangerous habit in the climate of the Church today. The Holy Spirit will have to work overtime to elect him.

John Allen thinks it will be the Archbishop of São Paulo, Cardinal Claudio Hummes, who is a moderate and a healer. The South Americans and the rest of the third world think it's time for one of their own and probably have the votes to make such a choice, but I doubt that they have the organizational skills to put together a coalition. The Italians talk of Tettamanzi of Milan, a fat and jovial man who seems to be able to keep everyone happy, whether it be the far right of Opus Dei and the Legionnaires of Christ or the moderate St. Agedius community. Because he is fat and jolly he is compared to John XXIII, which may be ludicrous but is typical of the quality of current speculation. Others speculate on John Baptist Re of the Congregation for Bishops. But can the Italians create a coalition of Europeans to support a candidate of their own? Cardinal George of Chicago thinks that out of courtesy the Sacred College ought to consider an Italian possibility before anyone else. After a quarter century of a "foreign" papacy, a return to the Italian style might be reassuring. A candidate elected because of his skin color or his geography seems a great risk.

One must not count out the two German dynamos — Kasper and Lehmann, the latter passed over for the red hat by the present Pope a couple of times. They are capable of putting together a coalition, but it would probably not have enough votes to elect a non-Italian European, a man who comprehends the crises in the Church and will address himself to the taming of the Curia.

The right-wing "movements" will lobby vigorously because their future depends on the next Pope. Neither Opus nor the Legionnaires are popular with all the bishops. In a less favorable papacy than the present one they could be in serious trouble. Father Maciel Degollado, the founder of the Legionnaires, would be suspended for credible charges of sex abuse if he were an American priest. John Paul has protected him. The next Pope may not.

Given the archaic style of a papal election, almost anything can happen, and we will have to live with it. This crowd of cardinals might easily make an even worse mess than the current one. One would not go far wrong, as the Irish say, to bet on a Pope who will be a nice, holy man who tries to keep everyone happy. Then again, such a man could be torn apart by the currents of anger and disappointment that sweep through the Church.

I'm in a dyspeptic mood. I want a man who can restore the élan that flourished immediately after the Second Vatican Council. Looking at the current front-runners, I can't expect that. But as Pope John and the current Pope prove, the Sacred College often does not elect the man they thought they elected. One can never tell beforehand what kind of Pope the man who emerges on the balcony to tumultuous cheers will turn out to be.

On the other hand, the dictum of "constitutional elections" elaborated by English scholar Owen Chadwick, which states that the successor will always be different from his predecessor, stands the test of the past several centuries. One can be fairly certain that the new Pope will be different. How different and in what directions remains to be seen.

ROME, NOVEMBER 12, 2003

How crucial is the upcoming conclave? Having survived somewhere between fifteen hundred and nineteen hundred years, depending on how you want to count, and having survived many disastrous Popes, the Catholic Church is hardly in serious jeopardy. Despite the turmoil in the Church since the Second Vatican Council, most of its members remain loyal to the tradition and the heritage, if not to its institutional leadership. It seems to be difficult to drive Catholics out of the Church.

Although most of the cardinal electors will not be able to admit it even to themselves, it is the credibility of the papacy that is at stake. John Paul II may have been hailed as one of the men of the century by *Time* magazine. He may have, as English historian Eamon Duffy has written, raised the Church to heights of prestige it has never known in the past. He may even receive credit from some for bringing down the communist empire. However, Catholic laypeople around the world, loyal to their heritage and accepting the central truths of their faith (such as the existence of God, the divinity of Jesus, the presence of Jesus in the Eucharist, and life after death), simply do not look to the papacy any longer for religious and moral leadership. They cheered for the Pope when he traveled around the world, but whether the issue be birth control or immigration, they pay little or no attention to what he teaches.

The cardinal electors ought to be concerned about electing a man who will be capable of winning the hearts and minds of the Catholic laity (and the lower clergy, who are generally on the laity's side). The papacy needs an occupant who will restore religious credibility to the office. While there may be men in the Sacred College who would do this, it is unlikely they will be elected Pope. The papacy needs another John XXIII if the credibility of the office among the laity and the junior clergy is to be recaptured.

To put the matter somewhat differently, the issue is still what it was in the last three papal elections: the Second Vatican Council. Although an ecumenical council can hardly be repealed, there are people in the Church who were so horrified by its effects that they have tried for all practical purposes to reverse it. It is no secret that they have had enormous influence during the papacy of John Paul II. The Pope says he is committed to the council, as properly understood. To implement it properly, as he sees it, it was necessary to restore order and discipline and a strong papal authority.

He did so and is applauded for it both by Catholic conservatives and by many non-Catholics, such as the editors of *Time.* He did so in great part, one suspects, because of the chaos he saw in the Church. But one cannot close the windows after they have been opened. The energies Pope John released with his *aggiornamento* (updating) cannot be put back in the box. To restore the internal credibility of the papacy, the next Pope will have to rediscover those energies and, discreetly of course, unleash them again. I doubt that this will happen. More likely the next Pope will make some minor modifications in the style of the papacy but little in the substance. It is hard to imagine a more effective recipe for disaster.

The code word that will be used by the minority of cardinals who would like the energies of the Vatican Council restored will be "pluralism." It means that the papacy can afford to trust local bishops and national hierarchies to make decisions that are appropriate for their cities and countries — as the local bishops did for a thousand years and more when poor transportation and nonexistent communication made a centralized, absolutist papacy impossible. To put the matter differently, they want the Roman Curia to work for the bishops instead of vice versa. They would argue that a delegation of power would enhance rather than weaken the credibility of the Vatican.

Will that mean more chaos? The answer these men would make is that you can't have a real and lasting reform in the Church without there being some chaos. Morever, the attempt by Pope John Paul II to put the cork back in the bottle has in fact made the chaos worse, because now it is underground. The local leaders, deprived of discretion in decision making, have lost control of their laity and clergy. It is time, say the advocates of pluralism, to try a new strategy.

Do they have any chance of carrying the day?

Practically none.

"It is unfortunate that the laypeople have lost their faith," one Italian cardinal said gently. "In the second and third world people still believe."

That was thirty years ago. Now I have discovered in conversations with well-informed Curia watchers that this casual dismissal of Western Europe and the English-speaking world is rooted in an ideology that has substantial influence here. The Vatican Council, they will tell you, was an important event. Unfortunately, it happened during the turbulent 1960s and was caught up in the revolutionary moods of those times. The "secularized" Catholicism that emerged will not survive. It is regrettable that the Catholic faith will die in these parts of the world. The Church, however, has had a long life. It understands that the faith has always been stronger in some places than in others. It is necessary, therefore, to return to the times before the council and build from there. Thus Catholicism will survive in the West only in "movements" like Opus Dei and the Legionnaires of Christ, which will lead the revival later this century.

This analysis is neat and seamless. It has many advantages — foremost, absolving the people who offer it from any responsibility for the present crises in Catholicism. What has happened is the unfortunate result of historical forces beyond their control. It further absolves them from any effort to reclaim the Church's credibility in the "secularized" West. It is sad, but there is nothing to be done.

The only problem with the analysis is that it is wrong; one might almost say criminally wrong. It is also, and this is worse, ignorant. Catholicism in the United States and in Ireland flourishes at the parish level. Moreover, Brazil, the largest third-world country, is permeated by pagan syncretism and under assault by evangelicals. Sexual attitudes of Catholics in Poland, the most important of the second-world countries, barely differ from those of American Catholics. In fact, a 1998 survey by the International Social Survey Program demonstrated that the decline in acceptance of the Catholic sexual ethic recorded in the United States is reflected in most Catholic countries.*

The loss of credibility of the Vatican is a worldwide problem. Isn't it obvious that the marchers and protesters of the 1960s were only a fraction of the population of Catholics in the West and that most Catholic laity were not swept up in the unrest? Finally, can we doubt that the Second Vatican Council, under the inspiration of the Spirit, came at a time of the Spirit's choosing?

---

*See Appendix A, "'Hypersexualized' Americans and the Second and Third Worlds."

Moreover, this theory has its years wrong. The "confusion of the laity" on birth control did not follow the disorders of 1968 but came several years before, when Pope Paul established his birth control commission to remove the question from the floor of the council, apparently not trusting his fellow bishops to discuss it. If there was a possibility of change — and why not, if one establishes a commission? — then there would be change. Or so American Catholics decided in those years when the Mass had changed so dramatically and change seemed to be in the air.

As I stand in the plaza of St. Peter's my vision blurs and I see once again the streams of purple-clad prelates pouring out of the basilica in late morning during the council. I sense again the excitement of those years. It was the springtime of the Church, the beginning of a new era of vitality and hope. The Church had proven wrong those who said that it should not change, would not change, could not change. The leadership of the Church faced a frightening mix of opportunities and challenges. It was a *chairos*, a decisive time. The leadership blew it.

In the decades that followed, the Curia reasserted the power it had lost to the council, reimposed its rigid control, and stifled the hopes of my generation of clergy and laity. A sour bitterness replaced those hopes. The failure of Catholic leadership to seize the opportunities, even to perceive them, is one of the great tragedies in the history of Catholicism.

The Church at the time of the council was open, expansive, self-confident, attractive. Now it has become narrow, rigid, frightened, and unappealing. Heaven forgive those who are responsible.

I do not necessarily dispute the curialists' good intentions, though I wonder whether one of their motivations was to protect their own power and their own careers. They have succeeded in squelching the promise of the council, but their own power is illusory. Most of the Catholics of the European and the English-speaking world no longer pay any attention to them. Yet it is unthinkable to many of the current curialists that they should ask whether they have made any mistakes or even wonder, in the phrase from the council they hate, whether they may have missed the "signs of the times." It is much easier and much more satisfying to blame the atmosphere of the 1960s and the laity of today. The next Pope may want to change the atmosphere here — or he may be part of it. Or he may not be able to change it all.

ROME, NOVEMBER 14, 2003

According to the news yesterday, the American bishops have decided to issue a pastoral letter on birth control. Here in Rome I hear various theories about the impact of the Second Vatican Council on the sexual attitudes of Catholics, most popularly that the council was necessary but it came at the wrong time — during the revolutionary unrest of the late 1960s. Therefore, it is now necessary to go back to the time before the council and begin again the work of renewal.

As a sociologist, I want to respond by analyzing the data we have. Here I will rely on three data sets, all representative probability samples:

- The National Opinion Research Center's Catholic school studies from 1963 and 1974

- A 2002 study by the Knowledge Network that replicated some of the items of the Catholic school studies
- NORC's General Social Survey from 1972 to 2002

Of course, the first hurdle I face in applying a sociological approach is that Catholic conservatives — lay and clerical — refuse to take sociological research on Catholics seriously unless it concentrates on "good" Catholics. The rest, a *massa dannata* of "not-good" Catholics, do not have the right to vote on Catholic issues and problems. However, the sociologist who defines as a Catholic anyone who says he is a Catholic can find some support in canon law, which says that a baptized person who has not formally apostatized or has not joined another religion is a Catholic. Perhaps the question of who is "good" should be left to God, the only one capable of reading the human heart. If the conservative retreats to the category of "practicing Catholic," the sociologist must observe that canon law does not know the term "practicing" as a modifier of Catholic. If the conservative then says that she means Catholics who attend Mass every Sunday, then the sociologist has a measure to see how different "good" Catholics (those who attend Mass every week) are from the rest of the Catholic population.

The birth control issue is the most pernicious controversy the Church has faced in the last half century. It pits the Vatican and the hierarchy (often less than enthusiastically) against the lower clergy and the laity. With the development of the contraceptive pill just before the Second Vatican Council convened, there was hope that the Church might approve it as a legitimate birth control technique. The fathers of the council wanted to debate the issue, but Paul VI removed the subject from their agenda and increased membership in the commission John XXIII had established to examine it. Married people and lay scholars were added to the commission. The issue was broadened from the pill to include all forms of contraception. Much to everyone's surprise, the commission voted to support an elaborate rationale of reasons for change. They had given the Pope what they thought he wanted.

A peculiar series of events followed. Leading officials of the Roman Curia, who had always criticized Pope Paul and had been responsible for his dismissal from the Curia, began a campaign against the decision of the commission. The Pope, they argued, was betraying the teachings of Jesus and the Church. For reasons of his own personality, Pope Paul had always wanted to please these enemies. For two years after his report, he hesitated. In the meantime copies of the report appeared in the world press. The Catholic laity and lower clergy took it for granted that the demographic, medical, and social reasons for the change constituted solid arguments and that change would occur when the hesitating Pope finally made up his mind. So the Catholic laity decided that artificial birth control was not sinful — a full two years before the student protests of 1968.

Then the Pope issued the encyclical *Humanae Vitae*, which indeed described the reasons for changing the birth control policy, but dismissed them without refuting them. The Church simply could not change its condemnation of birth control. The confused laity argued that if the Church could change Friday abstinence and the language of the liturgy and its relationship with Protestants, why couldn't it change on birth control? The responses then and now have not had any impact on them.

Pope Paul was so astonished by the reaction around the

world to his encyclical that he never wrote another one and indeed considered resignation. It was reported that John Paul I considered a revision of the teaching before he died. John Paul II, however, has reinforced the teaching by arguing that artificial contraception interferes with the perfection of the marital union between husband and wife, an argument that has changed few lay minds.

Recently American bishops have renewed the argument against birth control, a curious phenomenon in which aging celibate males who have been unable to control the sexual life of abusive priests apparently believe that they can reassert their control over the sexual lives of married laypeople.

As I have argued in my book *The Catholic Revolution: New Wine, Old Wineskins, and the Second Vatican Council,* the birth control issue emerged just as the changes initiated by the council were destabilizing the structures of the post–French Revolution Church. The documents of the council were moderate statements, but the implications of these documents suggested that change was possible on other matters, too. The legitimacy of change in the Church was the revolutionary event of the council. Moreover, matters that were once taught under pain of mortal sin were no longer considered sinful. You could disagree with the Pope and still be a good Catholic, people thought.

Arriving on the heels of such widespread destabilization, the reaction of the laity and the lower clergy to the birth control encyclical created a permanent divide in the Church between the Vatican and the lower ranks of the faithful. It also seems to have led to many other events. Weekly church attendance as measured by the annual Gallup surveys had *increased* in the years after the council and began to decrease after 1968. There had been few defections from the priesthood or the religious life before 1968, but after that year came a flood tide, not so much as a direct result of the encyclical, but because the encyclical had increased the destabilization of the old Church structures. The heady new wine of change had burst the old wineskins.

The sociologist cannot make theological judgments on the issue. He cannot approve or disapprove of either the birth control ban or the rejection of the ban. But he can and must say the ban in all its recent forms has not had the slightest impact on either the lower clergy or the laity. He also can and must say that in the birth control debate, the sides have long since given up listening to each other.

The Catholic school studies that NORC carried out in 1963 and 1974 provided a perfect natural laboratory to measure the impact of the council and the encyclical on Catholics. In 1963 55 percent of self-identified Catholics thought that birth control was always wrong. Even then almost half of the laity rejected the birth control teaching. In 1974 only 15 percent thought it was always wrong, evidence of revolutionary destabilization of Church structures. In 2002 data collected by the Knowledge Network showed that all the efforts of the previous thirty years to enforce the birth control teaching had failed. Fourteen percent of Catholics believed that birth control was always wrong. The repeated attempts of Church leaders to enforce the doctrine had failed, not only in the United States but in every Catholic country on which data are available.

Clearly the lower orders did not accept and do not accept the birth control teaching. Whether this constitutes a theological "nonreception" is a matter for the theologians to argue. The theory of reception is based on the notion of the earlier Church that a teaching requires *consensus totius populi christiani* — the consent of the whole Christian people. Those who endorse this idea do so very quietly today, because it is an area in which one can get into serious trouble. Can rejection by the laity cancel out a papal decision? The sociologist cannot say.

However, the sociologist can address the question of whether the "good" or "practicing" laity do accept the birth control teaching. They are the only ones, it is argued, whose reception is required.

There is indeed a correlation between frequency of church attendance and the belief that artificial birth control is always wrong. Twenty-six percent of "practicing" Catholics do "receive" the teaching, while only 8 percent of other Catholics "receive" it. However, more to the point, more than seven out of ten of "practicing" do not "receive" it.

To this unpleasant fact the conservatives respond that the only good Catholics are those who attend Mass regularly *and* accept church teachings. Such a response gives the game away. By this standard, the sociologist can study only those whose answers to his questions are already a given. To research the attitudes on birth control of only those Catholics who already accept the teaching is a waste of time. Moreover, it would exclude 85 percent of the Catholic population.

One might have thought that the changes were mostly among younger respondents, those still in the childbearing years. However, there were dramatic changes among those born before 1920, most of them in their sixties and seventies by the time of the second parochial school study — people who, notably, were least likely to have been swept along by the enthusiasm of the rebellious youth at the end of the 1960s.

Catholics at every age level changed their minds on birth control, despite the encyclical *Humanae Vitae* and in some sense perhaps because of it. Instead of docilely accepting the Pope's teaching (as he apparently had expected they would), they turned against the teaching and against the whole Catholic sexual ethic.

In the early years of the twenty-first century, fewer than half of "practicing" Catholics think that premarital sex is always wrong. Weekly church attendance does have an impact on sexual attitudes, but not an impact that eliminates sexual dissent from the "practicing" population. Moreover, the change among the older birth cohorts (born before 1930) demonstrates that many of those past the age of youthful passions no longer believe in the sinfulness of premarital sex. Thus the Catholic sexual revolution applied not only to birth control but also to premarital sex. Communal Catholics — those who are still Catholic but on their own terms — were born of the destabilization instigated, however unintentionally, by the council and aggregated by the birth control encyclical.

Nor was it the political unrest of the sixties that caused Catholics to turn away from the Church. In the thirty years from 1972 to 2002, disapproval of premarital sex by all Catholics has fallen in half — from 40 percent to 18 percent — while it has not changed among Protestants. If the social and political unrest of the late 1960s and early 1970s was responsible for the Catholic decline, why wouldn't it have led to a similar decline among Protestants? The alternative explanation — a revolution unique to Catholicism, caused by the impact of change in a Church that was not supposed to change — seems much more likely.

Again the sociologist must not be interpreted as approving

of premarital sex, but he must report the facts: in thirty years, Catholics have rejected several connected items of the Church's sexual ethic, despite the warnings from Rome and local bishops.

There has also been a more recent change in Catholic attitudes toward sexual relations between members of the same sex. While the judgment that homosexual sex is always wrong has declined somewhat among Protestant Americans since 1990, it has declined much more sharply among Catholics — from more than 70 percent to less than 50 percent. Catholics are now somewhat more than 20 percentage points less likely to be antigay than are Protestants. Those elements of the gay community that have been vehemently and sometimes violently anti-Catholic have yet to discover that what cardinals say is not what ordinary Catholics believe.

Again, if the revolutionary episodes in secular society thirty to thirty-five years ago are to be blamed for the decline of Catholic opposition to homosexual sex, then one must ask why the same phenomenon did not affect Protestant attitudes.

These numbers, it might be argued, do not show the attitudes of "practicing" Catholics — those who attend Mass at least once a week. Weekly church attendance does affect Catholic acceptance of Church teachings. (Or, more likely, attendance is affected negatively by disagreement with the teachings.) Even so, 65 percent of "practicing" Catholics do not think premarital sex is always wrong, and 30 percent do not think that homosexual sex is always wrong.

The proposition that the timing of the Second Vatican Council caused Catholics to turn from the Church's authority is one of the Vatican's urban folk tales. It serves the purpose of soothing any doubts or unease that curialists may have about the future of the Church or their own responsibilities for the present condition of the Church. The data mined for this analysis are unlikely to deprive the conservatives or reactionaries of the comfort the folk tales provide. One does not readily give up on one's myths.

GRAND BEACH, MICHIGAN, NOVEMBER 15, 2003

As we approach the next conclave (whenever it might be), there is reason to wonder why the situation within Catholicism seems so grim, in terrible contrast to the hope and joy that marked the successful completion of the Second Vatican Council. What went wrong?

In reading the first two volumes of the magisterial history of the council edited by Giuseppe Alberigo and Joseph A. Komonchak and the brilliant doctoral dissertation of my colleague Melissa Jo Wilde, I was struck by the fact that both Cardinals Montini and Wojtyla (Popes Paul VI and John Paul II) were conciliar liberals, as was Cardinal Ratzinger. How then did they come to roll back, or try to roll back, the world they helped to create?

Why has "collegiality" of Pope and bishops virtually ceased to exist? Why did Papa Montini fear to consult the bishops of the world about birth control? Why did Papa Wojtyla ignore the bishops on the issue of the ordination of women? If collegiality does not apply to these issues, what good is it?

Why have ecumenical efforts bogged down in frustration and anger?

Why, despite the document on the Church in the modern world,* of which he was one of the principal architects, has the present Pope seemed to despair of the modern world?

Why does the Roman Curia continue to lord it over the residential bishops?

Why do the Pope and Cardinal Ratzinger now use the conciliar documents as sources for "proof texts" taken out of context in a plea for the "real" spirit of the council?

I return to my theory of "destabilization" caused by the conciliar documents themselves. Once the unchanging model of Catholicism faced changes in liturgy, in scripture interpretation, in theories of religious liberty, in attitudes toward the Jews, in trust of the modern world, and in attitudes toward other Christians, its structures collapsed. The council fathers may not have foreseen this collapse, but they did vote for the changes (in overwhelming numbers). Hence the documents themselves and the action of the fathers (presumably guided by the Holy Spirit) were responsible for the destabilization.

Both Paul VI and John Paul II (and Cardinal Ratzinger) lost their nerve. The council had not intended massive defections in the priesthood or the religious life, so when the new freedoms created by the destabilization of the old structures made it possible for unhappy priests and religious women to abandon their vocations, it was necessary to slow down the energies of change at work and restore some kind of order, discipline, obedience, control.

---

*Gaudium et Spes, or Pastoral Constitution on the Church in the Modern World.

These attempts have inevitably failed because they presume that the nineteenth- and early-twentieth-century structures still exist. It is a strategy not unlike that of the Persian king who lashed the Bosporus because it destroyed his bridges — and about as effective. The result is that the new structures of Catholicism are emerging and have emerged with little reference to hierarchy and the papacy. Policies designed to restore order have created more disorder. In the name of curtailing a runaway "Spirit of Vatican II" (which often had little to do with the actual work of the council), the leadership has instead given impetus to that so-called spirit.

It is likely that once-liberal leaders such as Montini, Ratzinger, and Wojtyla did not realize how problematic were the structures of nineteenth-century Catholicism, how quickly they would collapse once change was permitted. On discovering that collapse, they decided to stop the change or at least slow it down, but it was too late. They had destroyed the structures of their own credibility. If, for example, women left the religious life in massive numbers and no new recruits replaced them, the reason was not materialism or feminism but that the rigid structures of the religious life itself were so weak they could not survive the winds of change.

To be fair, no one realized the potential frailty of the so-called confident Church of the 1950s, neither in America nor round the world. A push from a handful of conciliar documents and the whole house of cards collapsed. For many leaders who had known the seeming serenity of the preconciliar church, it was unthinkable that the structures had disappeared overnight. They reached back for these old structures to prevent a disappearance that had already occurred.

An abiding problem in the Roman Curia and most of the Church's leaders is the substitution of personal opinion for serious analysis of the Catholic world and its concerns. Often such opinions are daydreams that have little relationship to reality.

Thus Joseph Ratzinger, the head of the Congregation for the Doctrine of the Faith, once called the Holy Office, and previously called the Holy Office of the Inquisition, is surely the most important Catholic theologian of the last hundred or so years. One of the great intellectual architects of the Second Vatican Council, he subsequently turned against his own work and now has in effect directed the Pope's attempt to return the Church to the organizational structure that existed before the council. Ratzinger summarized his project when, speaking of the removal of Hans Kung's license to teach Catholic theology, he said, "The Christian believer is a simple person. Bishops should protect the faith of these little people against the power of the intellectuals." This ethos dominates Rome today.

Such pseudopopulism is common here in Rome. The curialist is proud of his defense of ordinary people against the bad guys — intellectuals, theologians, liturgical reformers. Unfortunately, Ratzinger was wrong on several issues in his judgment about Kung (made before Ratzinger became head of the Holy Office).

The "simple, little persons" don't read theologians. Indeed, hardly anybody reads theologians — especially German theologians — priests and bishops included. Theologians rarely matter to anyone but other theologians. Hans Kung's major offense was that his books actually sold, a rare phenomenon indeed for theologians. But they were not read by simple, little people. Kung, a Swiss intellectual, was read by other intellectuals (of whom there are large numbers in the Church, even in Ratzinger's native Bavaria). Such folk are more likely to be oppressed by the suggestion that they need the cardinal to protect their faith — and they certainly would not be dissuaded from reading Kung by the fact that his license to teach Catholic theology in the University of Tübingen had been revoked.

In fact, anyone who has observed envy among academics, especially among priests, and more especially priests who are also German theologians, might wonder whether Kung's real offense was that ordinary, well-educated Catholics actually read his books and made them bestsellers.

Mortal sin!

So the "simple, little" laypeople whom Kung oppressed were a fiction of Ratzinger's imagination: a useful fiction, because protecting them made him feel good and because they were a useful pretext for putting Kung in his place.

I don't question Joseph Ratzinger's good faith. Doubtless he honestly believes that the "simple, little" people, such as these may be, need protection. My point is that he was engaging in dangerous self-deception, the kind that ought to be intolerable among those who occupy central roles in the Catholic Church.

Similarly nearsighted, the local folk in Rome who blame the sex abuse crisis in the United States on the Jewish media (punishing the Church for its support of a Palestinian state) are guilty of anti-Semitism and monstrous and intolerable ignorance about the United States. They blame Bishop Wilton Gregory for permitting victims of abuse to lecture bishops and for advocating administrative solutions rather than canonical trials.[*]

*Bishop Gregory (now head of the Archdiocese of Atlanta) is president of the U.S. Conference of Catholic Bishops.

If they knew anything about the United States, they would grasp that such decisions were critically important and that they ought to be grateful to Bishop Gregory for his courage to do what had to be done.

The Curia lives in a dreamworld, a world of fiction, indeed of fantasy fiction. It is to be hoped (but hardly expected) that the new Pope will replace such fiction with solid and responsible analysis of the laity's real questions.

The story of Jesuit theologian Jacques Dupuis demonstrates that the Congregation for the Doctrine of the Faith still operates with much the same injustice as it did when it was called the Holy Office. The CDF announced that it was studying his book *Toward a Christian Theology of Religious Pluralism** and thus immediately put his reputation in jeopardy. They studied him for a year and a half and, while they don't use physical torture anymore, emotional anxiety is the next best thing. Finally, Dupuis was summoned before the ultimate board — Ratzinger and his top two aides, one of them now Cardinal Bertone of Genoa. They had prepared a fourteen-point "denunciation" of his book, on which the Pope had already signed off. They would publish the denunciation the next day and they wanted Dupuis to agree that he had accepted it.

One of Dupuis's advocates (a man whose presence is required at these hearings, and a fellow Jesuit) fought back. Where in the book, he demanded, are these errors? I don't recognize any of them. The least you can do is document the pages on which they occur. After heated discussion, Cardinal Ratzinger agreed that they would cite the pages of the book in which

*Orbis Books, 1999.

dangerous theology was being proposed. The publication of the denunciation was postponed while they found the pages.

Only they were never able to find them. Dupuis had been accused of heresy for statements he had never written. Whoever had compiled the document against him had apparently spun the charges out of air.

This sort of thing can happen in secret courts.

Finally, after considerable wrangling, the CDF issued a "notification" of two segments in the book that needed to be "clarified" because the subject was a complicated one. The Pope signed off on the notification just as he had on the denunciation.

One could argue that in the end justice had been served, though no one from a common-law country would agree. The book had been saved. So had Father Dupuis — after months of anxiety. No one apologized to him. No one suggested that the gnome who prepared the charges be dismissed. No one pointed out that Cardinal Ratzinger ran a dangerously incompetent organization. The victim had no recourse to rehabilitate his damaged reputation. All right, he wasn't burned at the stake. He wasn't locked up in a dungeon. Yet a great injustice had been done, a justice unworthy of a Church that still endorses the teachings of Jesus.

But Father Dupuis had been prevented from troubling the "simple, little people."

As an epigraph for his new book *Christianity and the Religions* (in which he makes the corrections required by the notification), Dupuis uses the following quote:

The servility of the sycophants (branded by the genuine prophets of the Old Testament as "false prophets"), of those who shy from and shun every collision, who prize above all their calm complacency, is not true obedience. . . . What the Church needs today, as always, are not adulators to extol the status quo, but men whose humility and obedience are no less than their passion for truth: men who brave every misunderstanding and attack as they bear witness; men who, in a word, love the Church more than ease and the unruffled course of their personal destiny.*

The quote is from an article by Joseph Ratzinger.

GRAND BEACH, NOVEMBER 16, 2003

Is it equitable in an age in which democratic government is slowly and erratically but inexorably spreading around the world that sixscore men should make a decision that will affect, for better or for worse and most likely for worse, the religious lives of a billion people?

If the cardinal electors in the next conclave are so ignorant as to repeat the cliché that the Church is not a democracy and actually believe it to be true, then they are far too ignorant to be permitted to vote in such a momentous election.

Illiterate peasants and townspeople once participated in the election of the Pope. Now well-educated Catholic people all over the world are told that the election of the Pope is none of their business. They must trust the wisdom and virtue of the cardinal electors and the power of the Holy Spirit to guarantee them that a wise choice will be made.

*Orbis Books, 2002.

My research shows that the laity in overwhelming numbers favor a much more democratic Church, one in which bishops are selected by priests and people, national conferences of bishops have more power, the Pope has influential lay advisers, and more attention is paid to the religious problems of ordinary people.* For the first thousand years of Catholic history these wishes would have been taken for granted. Now they are often dismissed as revolutionary.

Those who know even a little bit of papal history might want to ask why, then, were so many monstrously unwise choices made in ages past?

Why is it true, indeed almost self-evidently true, that those who are to be affected by the outcome of an election should have some participation in it? Why did Saints Leo and Gregory not feel called upon to defend the wisdom of their dicta on the subject?

There are three arguments supporting a more democratic Church. The first is that it is an elementary human right to participate in the selection of your leader. The present mode of papal elections violates that right. Secondly, those whose cooperation will be required if a man is to be a successful leader are much more likely to be part of his consensus if they have participated in his selection. Thirdly, according to Catholic theology, the Holy Spirit is at work among the ordinary faithful just as much as she is at work among the leadership elite. Why shut off her influence wherever it might be decisive?

*Andrew Greeley and Michael Hout, "The People Cry Reform," *The Tablet* (international Catholic weekly, London), March 22, 1997.

Were the people of New York City and their spirit-driven insights adequately represented by a cardinal who thinks that Little League and soccer games on Sunday are a critical religious problem? Were the people of Boston and New York adequately represented by prelates who routinely reassigned priests who abused children?

Pope Paul VI considered a reform in which the heads of the national conferences of bishops from around the world would be added to the Sacred College for voting purposes. Such a reform, minor and modest, would have nonetheless broadened enormously the democracy of papal elections. Nervous and neurotic man that he was, however, Paul VI permitted himself to be talked out of the reform.

By cardinals, of course.

By the standards of the ancient Catholic tradition and practice, the present system of electing Popes is immoral and corrupt. Worse still, by the evidence of history, recent and not so recent, it doesn't work very well.

Despite the faxes and the computers that are obvious in curial offices, the institutional organization of the Catholic Church has not changed appreciably since the late eighteenth century, except that the Vatican is no longer responsible for the Papal States (a great liberation) and the Pope now appoints most of the bishops of the world. One could argue that the traditional shape of Vatican organization worked well enough a hundred or a hundred and fifty years ago. Yet the Church now stretches to the ends of the earth and is responsible for the religious life of at least 1.2 billion people. To attempt to govern it with the same structures that existed in 1850 would be like the United States trying to return to the governmental style of Andrew Jackson's presidency.

To a relative outsider like myself this observation seems self-evident. Yet no one in Rome seems ready to consider a drastic reform in which the "updating" of the Church would apply to the papacy, the Curia, and the international organization.

As I walked around Rome last week I pondered what a social scientist can say about the governance style of the Roman Church. Much of the Catholic world believes the Church does not need social science because it has the Holy Spirit. The tools of management science, therefore, are not relevant. Nor, because of its divine origin, does the Church need to apply to itself its own principle of subsidiarity (that nothing should be done by a higher and larger level which could be done just as well by a lower and smaller level). Such reasoning, based on simplistic faith and even more simplistic theology, makes the institutional Church purely divine and thus unaffected by any of the problems that beset other human institutions — though patently the Church is affected by all of them. This reasoning also blames all the Church's historical errors or mistakes on God — who must have been responsible for slavery, the Crusades, anti-Semitism, and the persecution of Galileo. Don't worry about the poverty of leadership, pious folk (including cardinals) tell me. God will not desert his Church. Yet all that was promised by Jesus was survival — the gates of hell will not prevail against it. Moreover, such arguments are the equivalent of saying that the divine personhood in Jesus made it unnecessary for him to eat or drink or sleep — or as far as that goes, to die.

Perhaps the most serious issue facing the next conclave is whether the present strongly centralized organization of the

Church can continue. The truth is that it doesn't work very well because the current structure is "flat." There is in practice no ordered hierarchy leading down from the Pope to the local bishops and no reliable flow of information from the local bishops to the Pope.

The Pope's span of supervision includes several thousand bishops. Corporate theory argues that the span of supervision of an executive should be no more than five and preferably as low as three.

The leadership structure of the Church has not changed much since it supervised only Europe and communicated by stagecoach over the Alps.* Now it must supervise the world. Moreover, the Pope reserves the right to reverse decisions made at lower levels. Thus, for example, even though the local bishops and the nuncio submit ternas (list of three men who are qualified for a given diocese) and the Congregation for Bishops submits the master list of three, the Pope still may, if he so desires, toss out any or all of these ternas and make his own choice. That is certainly within his rights under current canon law, but in some instances such a rejection of the upward flow of information leads to unhappy results.

Under such circumstances how does the Vatican know what's going on in the Catholic world? How does it know whether crazy things are happening about which it must take a stand? How does it know whether Catholicism in a given country is in a healthy or abnormal state? How does it know the truth about a specific problem in a specific Catholic country?

*See *Inside the Vatican* by Thomas J. Reese, S.J. (Harvard University Press, 1998), for a description of how the Vatican is organized.

The truth is that despite all the solemn expressions of wisdom in the Vatican about, let us say, the problems of the Church in the United States, the Vatican is clueless on the subject, not simply because of anti-American bias or because of stupidity (though one must not exclude those factors), but because there is no way for the leadership in the Vatican to acquire adequate information about the United States — or any other country.

The Pope does not need better information, the lapdog theologians of the Curia Romana will argue, because he is being advised by the Holy Spirit. Whether any given Pope may actually believe that he has direct and immediate access to the Spirit is not the appropriate question. The proper question is whether he acts as if he does. When a Pope asserts that a teaching is "definitive" because all the bishops in the world teach it (as the present Pope does), without having consulted with them, one has to wonder how he knows.

Much of the upward communication that does occur comes from complaints of the extreme conservative members of the Church. They write letters about the faults of a local bishop. Not having any other source of information, curial officials often engage in adversarial conversations with the local bishop in which he is presumed guilty until he proves himself innocent.

It took a long, long time for the Curia to realize the seriousness of the sexual abuse problem in the United States. It is not clear even now that it understands the problem is not limited to the United States. In the absence of better information, more careful research, and deeper understanding of the various countries in the Catholic world, curial officials are forced to fall back on vague generalizations. They do so not necessarily because they are malicious (though many of them share in the common

European hatred of America), but because they need some basis on which to make decisions.

The fog of misunderstanding and insensitivity that often seems to an outsider to shroud Vatican City is not necessarily the result of incompetence, but rather the result of an organizational structure that constrains men to grope in the dark when they must make important decisions. That happens inevitably in a "flat" organization. Whoever the next Pope is, he would do well to consider opening up communication and transforming the "flatness" of Church organization.

Another mark of good management style is the ability to govern collaboratively. Even though there has to be someone who finally makes the call, someone at whose desk the buck stops, he still should listen very carefully to his subordinates and take into account their advice and recommendations before he makes his decision. The old adage that two heads are better than one has at least this merit: the second head may see something that the first has not seen. It is not unfair to say that since the bishops went home at the end of the Second Vatican Council there has been little collaborative governance in the Catholic Church.

Each Pope has had his way of dealing with the Roman Curia. The Curia objected to Pope John's council, just as it had under Pius XII to the shadowy but powerful presence of Madre Pasqualina. Subsequently it objected to Pope Paul's chief of staff and more recently to the minimal attention paid them by John Paul. In fact, some of them have suggested, again in whispers, that the largely Polish group around the Pope acts like a kind of government in exile, temporarily living in the Vatican, but with little concern about what goes on there outside the fifth floor of the Vatican Palace, unless they are drafting a document that he has requested.

Neither Pope Paul nor Pope John Paul II has taken the triennial Synod of Bishops very seriously. The Synod in its present form was a Pauline compromise, an assembly of bishops with no control of its agenda and subject to curial supervision. While bishops may speak, they do not engage in active debate, and the propositions that are supposed to have emerged from their remarks often do not reflect what was said, much less the emphasis with which it was said. Indeed, when Archbishop John Quinn of San Francisco had the audacity to suggest that more dialogue with the laity on birth control might be appropriate, he was promptly put down by curial representatives. No new thought is wanted at these sessions and no serious collaboration. The Synod is the ecclesiastical version of the Potemkin village.

The flat shape of the Church and lack of collaboration are not, one can safely say, part of the essence of the Church. Their effects, however, overlap. Either one would prevent an adequate upward flow of information and the utilization of all available talent and insight. Together they freeze the Church in an arctic blindness. The Pope speaks on marriage with the serene confidence that he understands it. Yet if he wants to be heard by those to whom he is speaking, his chances, especially in the current depreciated state of the Vatican's credibility, would be much better if his listeners felt they had some input to his reflections.

As the most elementary dictum of management science puts it, all those should have an input to a decision whose cooperation will be necessary to implement it. To put it more simply, the top leadership should not only want to listen, not only try to learn how to listen (neither of which it is currently ready to do), it must also see to it that there exist effective channels of upward communication and institutions of collaboration at every level in the Church.

One must assume that the Spirit still blows whither she will and that the Holy See has no monopoly on her. Indeed, one of the primary roles of any bishop, including the Bishop of Rome, must be the discernment of spirits, the judgment of which voices must be listened to. However, without collaboration and subsidiarity, most voices cannot be heard, much less discerned. In fact, in present-day Rome the only discernment that takes place is at the Congregation for the Doctrine of the Faith, which judges theologies and theologians and seeks only to prevent dangerous heresies.

But most of the work of the Spirit is outside the realm of theologians (as much as such a thought might offend some of them). All other insights, intuitions, suggestions, experiences, that might be pertinent to the life of the Church and the welfare of its people are simply cut off by the absence of communication channels.

Neither Paul VI nor John Paul II was much interested in such information flow. To be fair to them, few of their predecessors in the nineteenth and twentieth centuries were much interested either. Nor, for that matter, are many other bishops or even parish priests. Who has to listen anyway?

However, it is an iron law of corporate bodies that he who does not listen cannot communicate. A CEO who does not listen and who is uninterested in information will run his organization into the ground. A Pope in the contemporary world who follows a similar strategy will not destroy the Church (that has been tried by earlier Popes and it hasn't worked), but he will weaken his credibility enormously. When the Pope speaks today, the whole world hears him, not just bishops and priests. The style and the substance of what he says must suit the audience. This does not mean that he should change Catholic doctrine, but he must not seem arbitrary and cruel in the way he propounds it.

A few examples will illustrate the problem. The world believes that the Church hates gays and women and marital sex. I don't believe that these judgments are true — though there are undoubtedly some Church leaders who are guilty of these opinions. In a striking turn from Saint Augustine, Pope John Paul at the beginning of his papacy praised marital love, though in the abstract rhetoric of his phenomenological philosophy. However, he renewed (and, according to some, strengthened) the birth control prohibition, arguing that artificial contraception interfered with the total self-giving of spouses in marital love. This argument bombed with Catholic married people, whose standard reply was "How does he know?" The answer is that the Pope knows not through any personal experience but by philosophical argument. His audience, married Catholic laity, are not likely to be swayed by such arguments. They merely confirm the suspicion that Catholic leaders — elderly celibate men — do not understand the role of sex in the married lives of the laity. Whether they do or not is not the point in the present context. The point, rather, is that when Church leaders do speak on the subject, they should be careful to demonstrate that they do understand if they want the laity to listen to them. At one time they did not have to exercise such care. Now and ever after they will.

So far, it must be said in all candor that no Roman document and no document of the American hierarchy has displayed such sensitivity. These official statements appear to keep alive the tradition of Saint Augustine that the laity should engage in sexual intercourse as rarely as possible and under pain of venial sin if they don't intend it to produce children. It is my impression that some prelates consider marital sex if not exactly sinful, then messy and somehow less than appropriate.

The human sciences, which the Church always endorses but almost always ignores, tell us that what is unique about human sexuality as compared to that of the other higher primates, is its bonding power. Human couples make love far more often than do other primates, not merely to have children, but because lovemaking is part of the complex choreography that binds them together through the tensions and strains and conflict and frictions of the common life. Human marital sex is not "animal," as it was often described by past theologians (and still believed to be by some). Animals engage in sex only at certain specific times and are generally not interested the rest of the time. Humans, on the other hand, make love often because the energies of their organisms (including their love for each other) impel them to do so. Marital sex sustains men and women through the agony and the ecstasy of their lives together. Those aspects of primate sex, in other words, which are uniquely human are designed for pair bonding.

I have yet to encounter any Church leaders who understand this. Certainly no Vatican documents grasp it. Pope Paul had the input of laity on his birth control commission. In his encyclical he simply dismissed their input without replying to it. Pope John Paul, with his theory of "mutual giving," dug the hole deeper. The laity all over the world did not listen, and they still do not listen.

A parallel breakdown exists on the subject of various techniques for increasing the possibility of conception. Laypeople simply cannot understand why a Church that forbids contraception so that people will have children also forbids their efforts to have children if they are apparently infertile. Cardinal Ratzinger replies with his usual sense of tact and consolation that no one has the right to children. My sociological argument here is not on either side of the issue (though the laity have certainly made up their minds, as have the majority of the lower clergy), but on the inability of the Vatican to do anything but offend by its use of insensitive language. That's what happens when the leadership of a Church of more than a billion people eschews subsidiarity and collaboration and acts like it has a monopoly on God's Spirit.

A similar situation exists on the subject of women, and not simply on the issue of women's ordination (which the Pope's attempt to definitively close has not in fact closed among either men or women). Church leaders from the Pope down to the local pastor seem unable to keep their mouths shut on the subject of the rights of women. The leadership often chooses a rhetoric that reminds many women of nineteenth-century Romanticism — a glorification of the "feminine" that seems designed to keep women in their place. Whenever the leadership chooses a woman to speak out on the subject, they almost always choose someone who will simply repeat the party line. All others are dismissed as "radical feminists." In fact, many, many Catholic women who are devout and active in their parishes hate the Church leadership, which they perceive as hating them. I use the word "hate" advisedly. Adequate communication upward, which subsidiarity and collaboration would have provided, might have prevented the bitter anger among many Catholic women. The Pope just doesn't get it, they say. Neither, I would add, does anyone else in a leadership position in the Church. Or if they do, they keep their mouths shut.

Finally, it often appears that the Vatican has lost its patience with gays. While admitting that gay orientation is inherent, not chosen, the Vatican seems offended by the advances gays and lesbians have made in the quest for human rights in the Western world. Documents on the subject, with their emphasis on the "objective disorder" (whatever that may mean) of homosexuality, seem unduly harsh, and warnings to Catholic politicians about the approval of permanent relationships between gays (or worse, gay marriage) seem based on an almost obsessive fear that gays are a threat to heterosexual marriage — though that threat is assumed rather than proved. (Very few, if any, Catholic politicians take their orders from the Vatican these days, which is another problem caused by the flat and centralized structure of the Church.)

There also seems to be little awareness in the Vatican that the tone and style of the denunciation offend not only gays but, in many Western countries, their relatives who love them no matter what their sexual orientation — as the Church ought to love them and as the God who created them certainly loves them. Moreover, this love ought to be neither patronizing nor apologetic. Yet there is no sign of such understanding in the documents that come forth from the Holy Office — only anger and contempt, most egregiously in the suggestion that adopted children of gay couples will be subjected to violence, a charge for which no one offers any proof beyond what appears to be homophobia. Nor is there any warning from Cardinal Ratzinger or anyone else that the persecution of gays is a serious and contemptible sin.

I am not suggesting that the Church ought to worry about politically correct rhetoric. I am suggesting that on the subject of gays the Church ought to be spiritually correct — these men and women are deserving of the same loving concern as are all other human beings. I doubt that anyone in the top leadership here in Rome has ever seriously listened to gays and lesbians or members of their families.

I have heard highly placed prelates say that no theory about gay sex is acceptable but that pastorally it is another matter. They mean that in pastoral contexts, priests may encourage permanent unions. I have never been able to understand this distinction. If something is right "pastorally," why isn't it right also in theory?

Finally, there is the problem of Vatican anti-Semitism. The Pope himself has vigorously denounced all forms of anti-Semitism, yet it continues to exist even within the Vatican dicasteries — the kind of "respectable," middle-class anti-Semitism that has survived in Europe even in the wake of Hitler and the Holocaust. When the sexual abuse crisis in the United States was being explained away in Rome, there were whispers that the problem was created by the Jewish media.

Cardinal Oscar Andrés Rodríguez Maradiaga of Honduras suggested that the crisis had been created by the Jewish-dominated media in America to punish the Church for recognizing the Palestinian state. There was no rebuke from anyone in the Vatican and no outcry from the Catholic press anywhere. He is still on everyone's list of *papabile.* All we need is another Pope who can be called anti-Semitic. Someone here said to me that the Vatican couldn't care less about that. *Plus ça change . . .*

I have argued in this reflection that the absence of subsidiarity has created an unnecessary insensitivity in the Vatican that turns off many Catholics and deeply offends many who are not Catholic. There is no argument in this context that the Church should change its position on marital sex, the role of women, and homosexuals. Rather, my complaint is that the style of rhetoric used on such matters is counterproductive and defeats the Vatican's purpose in issuing statements on these subjects.

How does one go about creating subsidiarity in the Church?

Return the Selection of Bishops to the Local Church   Would there be politics in such a system? Certainly there would be, but it is only pretense that politics is not involved in the present system, a politics of covert cronyism. Could the Holy Spirit work through such a process? Perhaps the Spirit could work more effectively than in the present system.

I make this recommendation despite my uneasy feeling that any archbishop elected in Chicago by this system would want to get rid of me. More to the point, I cannot imagine any of the likely candidates taking the forthright stand that Joseph Cardinal Bernardin and Bishop George did on the sexual abuse problem. More likely they would engage in denial to the bitter end. Democracy, *pace* Churchill, is a terrible system, but in the long run it works better than the others. Since most dioceses would select from among their own number, such a system would prevent an ambitious man from advancing by way of moving to a more important diocese, possibly with the goal of a red hat. The Church might also consider a limit of two five-year terms on bishops, as many religious orders do for their leaders. This policy could also apply to the Pope himself, the Bishop of Rome, but only if each Pope voluntarily promised to abide by it.

Some people have suggested that such a system might produce bishops who, as they say the Anglicans have, would ignore traditional teaching. Without wishing to involve myself in the discussion of the current Anglican problems, I would point out that the Pope still has the final say and that the Catholic laity and clergy are generally sane and sensible people — more sane and sensible than many of those who have played kingmaker in recent American Catholic history, such as Cardinal Bernard Law of Boston.

Give the National Hierarchy More Authority and Power This would rehabilitate the national hierarchy from Cardinal Ratzinger's attacks. It should be able to enforce decisions (made by some kind of supermajority) on all dioceses. It should have authority to make decisions in many matters without clearance from Rome, though the Pope would have the right to review any decision he thought was inappropriate or harmful to the faithful.

There also might be supranational synods — European, North American, English-speaking world — with clearly delimited powers. Also more local synods within a country — archdiocesan, for example. This process would force bishops to attend more meetings, but perhaps no more than they do now.

The Church should rehabilitate the international Synod of Bishops in Rome, give it canonical and theological status, free it from the domination of the Curia, and permit it to establish its own offices in Rome and its own agenda (perhaps subject to papal approval). A group of its members should be appointed interim representatives between meetings and be available for consultation with the Pope whenever he desires it — or perhaps whenever they should request it. Such a Synod would work only if a Pope (unlike the last two) was completely committed to consultation. However, the Synod, like a General Council, would have no authority over the Pope and no right to reverse any of his decisions. The Synod would be nothing more than a group of men who, under the inspiration of the Spirit, would discuss with the Pope problems facing the Church and to whom the Pope would (hopefully) listen with great attention and interest.

Note carefully that at no point in this vast structure is papal authority under question. The Pope might have to listen to a lot more people, some of them doubtless with absurd ideas. On the other hand, if he did not want to listen to them, he would not be forced to do so. Nor would there be any limitation on his right to micromanage any subsidiary institution in the Church, right down to the local diocese or parish, if he had reason to do so. My plan is not to put restraints on a Pope but rather to make available to him more information and better-informed advisers.

Reconsider the Conclave   The election of the Pope might be returned to the actual parish priests of Rome, or the base for the election might be made much wider (with the priests of Rome nominating the papal vicar for Rome). Some way must be found for the clergy and laity of the world to believe that they are involved in the choice.

Transform the Roman Curia   The problem with the Curia, as I see it, is not that it's too big but rather that its two thousand members are much too small a staff for advising the leader of a Church of 1.2 billion people. The Curia must be larger, better trained, more professional, and restrained in its ability to interfere in the problems of the Church which could be solved better at a local level. Terms of service should be limited to two five-year periods (or maybe only one) so that membership on a curial staff would not become a career for ecclesiastical advancement.

Finally, there should be a division of work based more on the section of the world than on subject matter. There should be specialists whose training and function are to understand the Church in all its distant extensions.

Church leadership should make every effort to prevent the common practice in the current Curia of drawing up elaborate a priori plans for the entire Church with little or no consultation with those who might be affected by the plans. A classic case is the recent GIRM — General Introduction to the Roman Missal. Jorge Cardinal Medina and his colleagues at the Congregation for Divine Worship share with their fellow liturgists around the world a propensity for spinning out of the air fussy rubrical reforms for what they think are crucial problems facing the Church — in this case lack of reverence at the Eucharist and a failure to distinguish between the priest and the laity. In fact, if they had attempted any serious empirical analysis (which is hard for liturgists because they know everything already), they would have found the serious liturgical problem is not the occasional lack of reverence or the almost nonexistent collapse of the distinction between clergy and laity, but the sad truth that the liturgy is boring, especially when it is marked by poor music and bad preaching. If the Congregation for Divine Worship were truly interested in improving the quality of the liturgy, it would launch a worldwide campaign for the improvement of sermons.

The plan I have outlined as a basis for discussion may be more cumbersome than the present structure. However, given the size of the worldwide Church, it seems necessary in the name of subsidiarity that more men and women be brought into the decision-making process, always reserving final decisions to the

Pope, who presumably will have much better information and advice than did recent Popes.

This program could not be implemented all at once. The Church would have to see what works and what does not work. While some of the proposed changes would require revisions of canon law — or perhaps a whole new code of canon law — and some theological reconsiderations, none of them, as far as I am aware, violate Catholic doctrine.

Yet the most serious failures of the Church since 1960 in the final analysis are due not to ill will or stubborn resistance to change, but rather to the failures of an organized institution to adjust to the administrative and managerial demands of a world church in a world culture.

Father Thomas J. Reese, a political scientist, summarizes the challenge in his book *Inside the Vatican:*

Church history teaches that there are periods of progress when the church responds with intelligence, reason, and responsibility to new situations. Periods of decline have also marked the church, when individual and group biases blinded people to reality, hindered good judgment, and limited true freedom. Although this is true of any organization or community, what marks the church is its openness to redemption which can repair and renew Christians as individuals and as a community. Despite their weakness and sinfulness, Christians have faith in the word of God that shows them the way, Christians have hope based on Christ's victory over sin and death and his promise of the Spirit, and Christians have love that impels them to forgiveness and companionship at the Lord's table. The future of the church and the papacy must be based on faith, hope, and love.

Father Thomas O'Meara, O.P., of the University of Notre Dame (in the December 2003 issue of *Theological Studies*) seems to say the same thing from a theological viewpoint.

Authority in an age of media and education risks being ignored when it makes striking claims that have a basis only in simple neo-Aristotelian or devotional phrases. In our age of realism words such as assistance [of the Holy Spirit] or charism can become a cliché or a myth. Contributions from the entire Church, from human psychology and social communication, realistic forms of teaching and conversation among bishops as well as a modern theology of the graced individual can preserve episcopal teaching from decline. Without a psychology of grace, an ecclesiology of the Body of Christ, and a spirituality of an individual bishop, church leaders, far from being viewed as teachers of God's revelation, will be seen as an isolated oligarchy, a gnostic priestly caste claiming (in a society of ceaseless education) access to special sources knowing God's will.

As a sociologist I cannot judge Father O'Meara's theological assertions nor the theological implications of Father Reese's concluding sentences. I don't imagine that Cardinal Ratzinger would be pleased with either paragraph. But I can say that the world episcopate does indeed appear today to be an isolated oligarchy, a priestly caste claiming access to "special sources knowing God's will." Only systematic reform of the worldwide ecclesiastical institution can change that appearance.

Chicago, November 17, 2003

As speculation grows about a papal election, one sees little concern for what the Catholic laity around the world might want in the next Pope. Who are the laity anyway? What right do they have to an opinion? The Holy Spirit can work through the College of Cardinals without any help from the billion or so Catholic laypeople. After all, didn't Jesus establish the Sacred College and give it the right to select the Pope? Doesn't everyone know that the Catholic Church isn't a democracy?

In truth, two of the most important early Popes would have thought that the present method of papal elections was gravely wrong — Leo the Great and Gregory the Great. The methods they prescribed for the election of bishops for all dioceses, Rome included, were summed up in the succinct Latin dictum *Qui praesidet super omnes, ab omnibus eligatur.* For those unfamiliar with the mother tongue, that means "Who presides over all must be chosen by all." If that's not democracy, I don't know what is.

Saint Leo said there were three necessary conditions for the valid election of a bishop (including the Bishop of Rome): selection by the priests of the diocese, acceptance by the people, consecration by the bishops of the province.

The Sacred College came along more than a millennium after these sainted gentlemen.

Research I did with Michael Hout and with scholars in six other countries shows that the Catholic laity hope for a new Pope who will be attentive to the realities of their lives and open to change. He should achieve these goals by giving autonomy to the local bishops, appointing lay advisers, returning to the practice of electing local bishops, ordaining women, and allowing priests to marry. If enacted, these reforms will make the Church a more pluralistic and democratic institution. Our analysis of representative national surveys of the Catholic laity in six countries — Spain, Ireland, Germany, the United States, Italy, and Poland — support this conclusion.* The younger and better-educated laity in each country lead the call for reform.

Catholics from a wide variety of nations in Europe and from the United States call for institutional reforms that will reflect the pluralism in the Church. Large majorities support changes that will open the Church in ways that will allow many voices to be heard. Through electing bishops, advising bishops and the Pope himself, and exercising some degree of local autonomy, lay Catholics could carve a more influential niche for themselves. They hope that the next Pope will accord them the opportunity.

Catholics also support changes in the clergy. They like the idea that priests might marry. In Spain, Ireland, and the United States, they support the ordination of women by a two-to-one margin. In Italy, a clear majority also agrees.

Against those tempted to dismiss these findings on the grounds that the Church is not a democracy and hence the cardinal electors need not consider the wishes of the laity, we offer

*See Appendix B, "What the Laity Want in a Pope — A Study in Six Countries."

the arguments of prudence and history. The Church is not now nor has it ever been embodied in the hierarchy. It is standard teaching that the people of the Church are the Body of Christ. Their concerns should carry enormous weight with those who would be their leaders. From history we know that local bishops used to be elected — in less democratic times. There may be arguments against the practice, but only those ignorant of history could suggest that an elected episcopate is foreign to the nature of the Church. Electing bishops and respecting their autonomy in matters of local concern would return the Church to an ecclesiastical administrative style taken for granted for over a thousand years.

Speaking from the perspective of sociologists, Hout and I are unable to respond directly to those who say that the election of the Pope is the right and privilege of the cardinals and is no one else's business. However, three observations of a sociological sort can be made:

1. No one could possibly claim that the right of the cardinal electors is part of the essence of the Church.
2. In the contemporary world those who are unhappy with the selection of a leader, any leader, are less likely to follow that leader, even if they do not formally break with him. Such a leader may reign, to be sure, but it will be harder for him to rule.
3. As we understand Catholic theology — and we are subject to correction by those more learned in these matters — the Spirit of God is present in the people as well as in the leadership. The leadership would be

imprudent, not to say arrogant, to dismiss the possibility that the Spirit might be speaking to them through the wishes and insights of the ordinary people.

The laity's preferences will have little bearing on the election of the next Pope, but a wise leader would take them into account all the same.

Today John Allen's weekly column "The Word from Rome" included a list of cardinals who are likely *papabile*.

- Francis Arinze (Nigeria), prefect of the Congregation for Divine Worship
- Jorge Mario Bergoglio (Argentina), archbishop of Buenos Aires
- Godfried Danneels (Belgium), archbishop of Mechelen-Brussels
- Ivan Dias (India), archbishop of Mumbai (Bombay)
- Cláudio Hummes (Brazil), archbishop of São Paulo
- Walter Kasper (Germany), president of the Pontifical Council for Christian Unity
- Norberto Rivera Carrera (Mexico), archbishop of Mexico City
- Oscar Andrés Rodríguez Maradiaga (Honduras), archbishop of Tegucigalpa
- Christoph Schönborn (Austria), archbishop of Vienna
- Dionigi Tettamanzi (Italy), archbishop of Milan

John told me last week in Rome that Hummes was his best guess. I don't trust Kasper. Rodríguez Maradiaga sounds like an anti-Semite. Schönborn is a reactionary creep. Tettamanzi is supposed to be a lightweight.

None of the rest except Danneels is impressive. I fear he is too impressive. And has a history of heart trouble.

My guess is that the next Pope will be a good and holy man who will try his best to heal the polarization in the Church. He is likely to be torn apart by both sides in those efforts. No one seriously wants healing. The right still wants (at least) the effective repeal of the Second Vatican Council, the excommunication of those who practice birth control, the dismissal of homosexual priests, the punishment of politicians who do not oppose abortion and gay rights, and (in some cases) an obligatory return to the Latin Tridentine Mass. The left wants the ordination of women, optional celibacy, the expansion of lay power, gender-inclusive language, and (in some cases) the recognition of abortion rights.

How large are these two groups in the American Church? If opposition to birth control is a fair measure of the conservative position, the right is no more than 15 percent of the Catholic population. The left is more difficult to measure because its boundaries are porous. For the sake of the argument let us postulate that the ideological hard left is also no more than 15 percent. Between the two are the vast majority of Catholic laity, who have no strong ideological feelings but have made up their own minds on sexual issues and on the credibility of Church authority and hence are hardly on the conservative side.

The right was overwhelmed by the council. Indeed, it is reported that the founder of Opus Dei considered taking his group into the Orthodox Church. However, the vacillation of Pope Paul and the quasi-restorationist policies of Pope John Paul gave them new hope, and they struggle to reassert the total influence on the Church that they think they once had. They will not be satisfied with a Pope who refuses them more power, much less one who tries to rein in their power. The left, to the extent that the *massa dannata* support many of their positions but without the fervent ideology, is more ambiguous and problematic. As a European cardinal once pointed out to me, the right goes into schism, the left just drifts away.

Yet the credibility of the papacy, it must be said honestly, has been weak among most Catholics since the Church leadership failed to adjust to the revolution of the council. Minimally, the left will need from a healing Pope the promise that the oppressive atmosphere they see in the Vatican will ease and that the papacy will be more open and more ready to listen. Yet if the Pope shows any signs of belief that reform is still needed in the Church (*ecclesia semper reformanda*) and that Pope John's window will remain open, the right will be furious. Moreover, such organizations as Opus Dei and the Legionnaires of Christ will fight bitterly for the preservation and enhancement of their power.

It must be said candidly that the new Pope will inherit a polarization that has been exacerbated by the policies of John Paul and that, unless he is an extraordinary man (and few such are observable), his attempts at healing will only make matters worse.

INTERLUDE

January 2004

The world looks very different from the shores of Lake Michigan than it does from the banks of the Tiber, save that in both Rome and the United States the disconnect between the leadership of the Church and the ordinary laity is increasing. I'm not sure that the next conclave — which probably won't happen for a long time — will even recognize this disconnect, apart from blaming the laity for their problems.

Catholic bishops in this country still don't get it. Their credibility has been devastated by the reassignment of sexual predators and the subsequent failure to remove bishops who did the reassigning. Yet eight of their number have proposed as a follow-up to the Dallas Conference and its "zero tolerance" for sexual abusers that there be a Plenary Council in the American Catholic Church, the first since the nineteenth century. At such councils, bishops enact laws for the laity and the lower clergy, though rarely for themselves. The last such council passed a law that the clergy should wear frock coats, a rule still on the books.

Such a council would "strengthen priests in teaching the gospel especially in regard to sexual morality so that we can give support to the lay faithful in responding to their call to holiness." They would, in other words, pressure priests to try to reimpose the birth control ban on the laity.

This goal reflects a conviction among conservative Catholics that the problem of sexual abuse has arisen in the United States because the married laity practice birth control and lower clergy do not denounce them. The logic of this argument is difficult to follow. How does the behavior of the laity in their marriage beds lead priests with serious personality disorders to prey on the young? How does the silence of the parish clergy on the subject of birth control account for the reassignment of abusive priests? There is no evidence to support such claims.

However, the argument is typical of the sweeping generalizations to which priests, bishops, and curial officials are prone — personal opinion as cultural analysis that requires no proof and is true by the very fact that one states it. The eight bishops propose that they and their fellows come together, get tough with lower clergy and the laity, reimpose the birth control ban, confirm their own "authoritative exercise" of ministry, and thus reestablish their credibility and deal decisively with the root causes of the sexual abuse problem.

Huh?

They lack the imagination to grasp that such a Plenary Council would become a mix of zoo and circus. It would make the Dallas meeting look like a minor blip on the radar screen. Reporters would swarm like flies on a humid day, each of them with a personal take on the proceedings, most of them inaccurate. Protesters would picket and demonstrate. Catholic dissidents would scream at TV microphones. Some bishops would make stupid and inept comments on camera because it is in their nature to do so. Critics would argue that, having protected the pursuit of sexual pleasure by priests, the bishops were now trying to deny or impede sexual pleasure for the married laity.

Some would also say that, having cooperated in the sexual abuse of the young and thus being guilty of serious sin, the bishops were in no position to make moral judgments about others.

Thirty years ago the lower clergy and the laity decided, rightly or wrongly, to reject the leadership's claim to control the sexual lives of the married laity. Since then, repeated demands for compliance have not worked and have often been counterproductive. A Plenary Council, like the one the eight bishops propose, would make the Catholic Church a laughingstock. Again.

ABC called my office the other day to make sure that I was around and accessible. Apparently there has been an announcement that the Pope will not do Holy Week services this year. However, it seems to mean only that he will not do them outside the Vatican.

An article in the *New York Times* this month hinted that Archbishop Stanislaus Dziwisz is the one who delivered the alleged papal endorsement of Mel Gibson's film on the Passion, which many Jewish leaders are saying is anti-Semitic.

A conclave, and another scandal, in the offing.

FEBRUARY 2004

The Catholic left would have us believe that the most serious problem the Church faces is clerical celibacy. If the Church would only ordain married men, the vocation crisis would disappear, the quality of preaching would improve, there would be no more sexual abuse, and bishops would have to change their style of leadership because the wives of priests would not tolerate their present behavior. Priests seem especially likely to see the abolition of celibacy as the solution to all problems and are furious if someone suggests that it is not all that simple.

The Catholic right, on the other hand, wants to blame everything on homosexuals. The sexual abuse crisis, they say, resulted from the ordination of large numbers of homosexuals from the easygoing seminaries after the Vatican Council. Homosexuals ran and may still run seminaries. Homosexual priests do not preach the traditional Catholic sexual ethic. They are the ones who are demoralizing the Church.

Bishops and Vatican officials seem to be among those most likely to blame Church problems on homosexuals.

Two major reports were issued this month — the report on prevalence and incidence of sexual abuse written by the John Jay College of Criminal Justice, and the report on the causes and contexts of sexual abuse written by the lay National Review Board. After the appearance of the reports, representatives of both left and right scurried around looking for sound bites and data bits that would confirm what they already knew to be true.

In fact, there was precious little evidence to support either side. If 96 percent of priests were not abusers, then celibacy would hardly seem to be the cause of sexual abuse. While 81 percent of abusers were homosexuals, it does not follow, except by twists of logic that the Catholic right and certain curial bureaucrats are incapable of avoiding, that all gay men or all gay priests are abusers. In fact, my own research[*] shows that some 16 percent of priests are gay and three-fifths of them have lived

[*]As reported in *Priests: A Calling in Crisis,* University of Chicago Press, 2004.

celibate lives (as opposed to four-fifths of heterosexual priests). Mature gay men seek sexual partners from among other mature gay men. Immature gays go after junior high school boys. Blaming homosexuals for the sex abuse crisis is part of a larger syndrome in which a certain proportion of American society (and of American Catholics) display their deep-seated hatred for gay men and women. Shame on them for not realizing that God loves them as much as he loves everyone else! Blaming gays for the problems of the Church (and society) is a sickness not unlike racism and anti-Semitism and anti-Catholic nativism, and it is characteristic of the same kind of twisted personalities as these other prejudices.

American Catholics will have to pick up the tab (perhaps eventually $1 billion) one way or another for the episcopal incompetence and malfeasance in office. It is not fair, it is not right. In the Catholic Church, as it is now constituted, that's simply the way it is.

Just as at one time we could not replace abusing priests, so now we cannot replace the bishops who created the abuse crisis.

April 2004

The bottom-line question in the wake of the audit of the Catholic bishops' efforts to prevent sex abuse is whether children and young people are safe now in Catholic environments. Perfectly safe? No. As safe as they should be? Not yet. Safer than they were before the bishops enacted their Charter for the Protection of Children and Young People a year and a half ago? Yes, indeed.

However grudgingly and reluctantly, most bishops complied with the audit and many improved their compliance by following the recommendations of the auditors. Kicking and screaming perhaps, they now have in place the institutions and mechanisms for controlling rogue priests. But the institutions and mechanisms are still new. It remains to be seen how smoothly they will work in practice. It also remains to be seen whether individual bishops will pursue their processes with vigor and enthusiasm. In short, the audit reveals a promising start — nothing more, but nothing less, either.

I will confess to surprise at how well most of the bishops co-operated with the former FBI agents who descended on their chancery offices throughout the last year. Bishops don't like outsiders, much less former federal cops, poking their noses into how they do their work. I would have expected more determined resistance to the audit. However, it is better to have former federal cops snooping around than local journalists — or tort lawyers.

Perhaps many of the bishops have come to terms with a climate in which they will no longer be able to cloak themselves in a mantle of secrecy. However undesirable the situation, they have begun to sense that they are now doing their work in the public domain. To use a metaphor from the New Testament, they have adjourned from the closet to the housetop.

There doubtless will be mistakes up there on the housetop. New games and new rules are hard to learn. Yet the charter and the audit suggest a major turning point in the history of the Catholic hierarchy in this country. They might not have wanted an audit by laypeople commissioned by a lay board, but their leaders were smart enough to know that it had to be this way, and the others went along, if in some cases only because they had no real choice.

It is a measure of the justified anger of the victims of abuse that they issued a strong critique of the audit before they could have read it and thus earned themselves equal billing in the media — whether their critique was valid or not. It is a measure of the bishops' lack of credibility that they are subject to such hostile spins on their work. Those among them who think they can now move beyond the sexual abuse crisis are kidding only themselves. Their credibility as a group is still at ground zero. If they continue their project of hassling the laity about birth control and Catholic politicians about gays, they will run the risk of being dismissed once more as hypocrites. The audit is both a step toward making the Church safer for kids and a step toward rehabilitating the bishops' credibility as religious leaders.

I am no fan of the hierarchy as a group (though I admire some of them), yet I must say that they have made a good beginning in taking these two steps. Now one can only hope and pray that the Vatican does not intervene to force them to reassign abusing priests, a move that would cut the ground out from under the American hierarchy's best efforts.

Does that mean that Catholics ought to trust their bishops? They should trust their own bishop to the extent that he has won their trust. It is no longer to be given automatically and as a matter of course. Bishops today (and parish priests, too) have to win the trust and respect of the laity. They may not like this change in the rules, but on reflection the more intelligent ones will realize that this is the better way.

Perhaps the best way to describe the hierarchy's current situation is that they have begun to pull themselves out of the hole they dug for themselves. How long and how hard they will pull remains to be seen.

I've been reading books by Francis Oakley, who, with his friend Brian Tierney, is an authority on the Council of Constance and the decree *Haec Sancta,* which asserted that a council could remove a Pope. The Council of Constance did just that, removing three claimants to the papacy, as a matter of fact. Oakley argues that the conciliarist theory of a balanced power between the Pope and a council is a form of constitutionalism that dominated the question up until 1870, when the imperial, absolutist papacy seemed to obliterate it from Catholic memory. Yet, he says, historians as opposed to theologians are insisting that Constance was viewed as a valid council in its own day and that the willful and deliberate forgetting of the past simply will not work.

I am persuaded from my own work that most of the conflict in the Church today and most of the loss is the result of an imperial papacy's inability to consult, to take counsel, to learn, and above all to listen. The only possible response to the destabilization caused by the Second Vatican Council was the collegiality that the council promised but Paul VI sidestepped by the vacuous Synod of Bishops. Finally, the losses in the church were caused by lack of collegiality. Only half the council happened — changes but no collegiality.

The Church today is more imperial than it has ever been before. And the new, hard-line bishops in Phoenix, Oakland, St. Louis, Newark, Philadelphia, and New York are clearly imperial bureaucrats who care only to win papal approval and could not care less about what their people think.

Some of the other bishops and some of the insanely ambitious young auxiliaries want a Plenary Council with which they can crack the whip and force the laity and the lower clergy back into line. They don't grasp that ever since the sex abuse crisis, no one listens to them. They figure they can get their power back by exercising it ruthlessly. It's dumb, but no one ever got to be a bishop by being smart. Sometimes the Vatican makes mistakes.

Thus both St. Louis and Boston threaten not to give Communion to John Kerry or anyone else who doesn't toe the line on abortion and homosexuality. A committee of bishops is looking into the matter and probably won't go that far. Yet no one seems to be considering a ban on Catholic politicians who support a preemptive war (which the Pope and the bishops have both condemned) or the death penalty.

Meanwhile Cardinal Edward Egan has gathered together a group of twenty-seven bishops (none with too much clout) to scuttle the National Review Board and the Compliance Office. We cannot permit those people to ride roughshod over us, the Alpine one informs the rest of the bishops.

When will it ever end? Not in my lifetime, surely.

MAY 2004

I subscribe to the consistent ethic of life that Cardinal Joseph Bernardin enunciated some years ago. I believe abortion is wrong. I believe the death penalty is wrong. I believe preemptive war is wrong. I also believe that we Catholics must promote this "seamless garment of life" — as the cardinal called it — by the methods of civilized discourse, not by attempts at raw political power, especially since the Church has yet to persuade most Catholics of this consistent ethic.

Thus I will take seriously the "pro-life" enthusiasts when they are ready to protest against the death penalty. I will take them seriously when they denounce criminally unjust wars. Otherwise, I have to wonder why some lives enjoy higher value than others. Life is, after all, life.

The current discussion among some bishops of refusing the sacraments to Senator Kerry for his stance on abortion does the work of the Republican National Committee for them. Are these bishops willing to deny the Eucharist to those Catholic politicians who support the death penalty? Are they willing to deny the Eucharist to those Catholic politicians (including Senator Kerry) who support the Iraq war? And if not, why not?

Moreover, do they intend to preach in season and out against the death penalty and against the war with the same vigor they apply to abortion? Will they tell Catholics that it is a sin to support an unjust war and to vote for a candidate who is responsible for such a war? And again, if not, why not?

I can think of a couple of reasons for this inconsistency. The first one is that denouncing abortion will get you attention in the Vatican, whereas attacking the death penalty and the war is not likely to promote your career. The other reason is that there are different rules for Democrats and Republicans. It is curious, to say the least, that thirty years after *Roe v. Wade* the issue of denying the sacraments would be raised during this election year.

Bishops also threaten political leaders who support civil unions between homosexuals. Given their tolerance for sexual abusers in the priesthood, that looks a bit hypocritical. I have never heard any of them criticize gay bashing. If you are a follower of Jesus of Nazareth, you cannot tolerate hatred for anyone, especially since the Church now teaches that the homosexual condition is not freely chosen.

Finally, some bishops have doubts about permitting women to participate in the washing of feet during the Holy Thursday services. These men are uneasy about women Mass servers. They will tolerate women distributing Communion only when it is absolutely necessary. Such sentiments will doubtless also promote their careers.

Yet, unless I've missed it, they haven't spoken out against rape. Between a fifth and a quarter of women in our country are rape victims. Why is the Catholic Church so silent on the subject? Why does Catholic leadership seem unaware of just how routine the abuse of women is — not merely at the service academies and in the military and on college campuses, but everywhere in our society? Why are they so obsessed with keeping women out of the sanctuary and so uninterested in the constant danger to women of their violation and the frequent fact of violation?

I realize that Church leaders from Peter and his colleagues on down through the centuries have not been all that brilliant or all that courageous. I understand that, with some exceptions, the current crowd are not much better. At least Peter and his bunch had the decency to apologize and admit their mistakes. The current crowd don't apologize much, and when they do, their contradicting actions destroy their credibility.

All right, gentlemen, the truth is that our faith is not in the hierarchy but in God and Jesus and the Catholic heritage. Is it foolish of me to wish you would do a little better job at bearing witness to what we believe?

June 2004

I don't know whom the Catholics in Colorado Springs are supposed to vote for. The bishop there has said that Catholics should be denied Communion if they vote for politicians who defy Church teaching by supporting abortion rights — implying, in this case, Democratic candidates. The Republican platform in the last presidential election also supported abortion in some circumstances. Perhaps the only course open for Catholics in Colorado is to go fishing on Election Day! However, it would be interesting to know how many votes will be affected by the ban. Catholics in the United States have a long history of rejecting clerical intervention in politics.

Nonetheless, the fringe of the hierarchy has been misbehaving. The bishop of Camden informs the governor of New Jersey that, should he show up at the bishop's installation, the bishop will deny him the Eucharist. Only problem is that there was no indication the governor would show up. The new bishop of New Ulm tells his diocese that his revered predecessor was guilty of teaching false doctrine and sends the offending book off to the Conference of Catholic Bishops to confirm his reading. Only problem is that the conference theologian can find no major problems in the book. The bishop of Brooklyn tells state legislators that same-sex marriage would be like marrying an animal pet. The archbishop of the military sacks without due process Father Tom Doyle, O.P., who was one of the first to warn of the pedophile problem. The archbishop of Boston engages in a Holy Thursday diatribe about baby boomers instead of offering to wash their feet.

Where did these guys come from? Never in my wildest moments could I come up with these high jinks for one of my stories. They're not typical, I hasten to add, but they're out there just the same, making the Church look terrible.

More seriously, the *stylus curiae* — which means the style of the Curia but also in a classic pun the dagger of the Curia — has done in the National Review Board, which was supposed to verify the hierarchy's compliance with the Protocols for the Protection of Children. Cardinals Egan and Rigali, men who spent most of their priestly lives in the Curia, stuck the dagger into the board by preventing its second-year review of compliance. The review wasn't exactly canceled, it was "delayed" — long enough that it wouldn't be done, a characteristic curial trick. Moreover, the death blow was delivered before the board even knew it was under attack. It was a slick job, not untypical of the Curia. The two cardinals proved themselves successful conspirators, apparently unconcerned that their plot would re-create all the doubts about how serious the hierarchy is in protecting children.

Why do it? To reassert their authority. Apparently they think that the way to recapture their credibility in the wake of the sex abuse scandal is to act like tough, nasty authoritarians. Instead of showing humility and openness and transparency (of which ex-curialists are incapable), they pretend that they are Renaissance princes.

Fed up with the endless hassle — and the mean, nasty letters they routinely receive from the fringe — four of the members of the Review Board are resigning in July. If the compliance review is not somehow salvaged, others will probably quit, too. The curialists will be delighted. Then they can appoint a new board that will do their bidding, like good Catholic laity should. Credibility? Who needs credibility when you have a red hat!

Such an outcome is intolerable. I have seen evidence that abusive priests are still in rectories. Many — perhaps most — bishops have done their best, but others have not. If the review board mechanism fails, there will be no guarantee that children will be safe in Catholic environments. The last two years' efforts at credibility will have been wasted.

Those who have resigned — Justice Burke and Messrs. Bennett, Burleigh, and Panenta — ought to withdraw their resignations and take on the red hats in public. The issue — responsible Catholic leadership — is too important to be side-tracked by ingenious little plots cooked up, if not exactly in the Vatican Gardens, in some similar place in the United States.

But what about the pro-life vote? Data from NORC's General Social Survey show that Catholics and Protestants differ little on abortion questions; large majorities think that abortion should be available when there is a risk of a defective child, a threat to the mother's health, or pregnancy caused by rape, while similar majorities reject the legality of abortion if the woman is unmarried or cannot afford another child or simply doesn't want a child. Only 4 percent of American Catholics are pro-life on all seven NORC items — and a third of those voted for Gore! One might argue that Catholics should oppose the availability of abortion in all circumstances. That may well be true, but in fact they do not.

A useful measure of the impact of such attitudes is the issue of abortion after rape. Twenty percent of Protestants reject the availability of abortion in such circumstances, as do 24 percent of Catholics. The latter group were ten percentage points less likely to vote for Mr. Gore than other Catholics were. The net loss of Catholic votes to the vice president therefore is 10 percent of 24 percent, or 2.4 percent. Since Catholics are approximately a quarter of the American population, one-quarter of 2.4 percent is six-tenths of 1 percent — the small amount that Mr. Gore's popular-vote victory would have increased if abortion had not been an issue for some Catholics. Moreover, these calculations assume that abortion was the only reason or the main reason that anti-abortion Catholics did not vote for Gore. So the impact of Catholic abortion attitudes on the last election might have been even smaller.

To paraphrase the first Mayor Daley, most Catholics do not vote on the abortion issue, and those who do have little impact. Sociologists cannot say whether Catholics should make abortion the only or the major issue in a presidential election. They can say only that most of them have not.

What, then, of the publicity created by the bishops who deny that Senator Kerry has the right to receive Communion, and by the bishop of Colorado Springs who avows that Catholics will lose the right to the sacraments if they vote for the senator? The ad hoc committee of bishops presided over by Cardinal McCarrick of Washington, D.C., is unlikely to endorse such draconian measures. Moreover, it is improbable that the Catholic hierarchy, disgraced and discredited as it is by the sexual abuse scandal, has the moral high ground to influence Catholic voters in any significant way.

July 2004

Catholics can vote for John Kerry. They don't have to, but it would not be a sin to do so. Or so one might conclude from the remarks of a distinguished theologian:

> A Catholic would be guilty of formal cooperation in evil, and so unworthy to present himself for Holy Communion, if he were to deliberately vote for a candidate precisely because of the candidate's permissive stand on abortion and/or euthanasia. When a Catholic does not share a candidate's stand in favour of abortion and/or euthanasia, but votes for that candidate for other reasons, it is considered remote material cooperation, which can be permitted in the presence of proportionate reasons.

These are not the words of some radical liberal Catholic theologian who is unconcerned about killing babies. Rather, they were written by the prefect of the Congregation for the Doctrine of the Faith, Joseph Ratzinger. It is as close to an official statement on the subject as one is likely to get. It says that Catholics are not obliged to vote on one issue, no matter how important the issue might be. They may vote for John Kerry "for other reasons" so long as they are not supporting him merely for his pro-choice stance.

That ought to settle the matter. Catholics who have been confused by the insistence of a few bishops, some priests, and some pro-life laity that they must vote against Senator Kerry now know that they are free — just as they always have been — to make their choice balancing all issues.

This theory of "remote material cooperation" is traditional Catholic moral teaching, however obscure and convoluted its use of language. Apparently the few bishops who excluded Catholics from Communion if they voted for Kerry didn't know much traditional moral theology — which demonstrates what the qualifications are for the bishopric these days.

The bishops of the United States actually quoted the paragraph from Cardinal Ratzinger (at the end of a memo he had sent them) in the documentation with their recent statement on the subject.

Moreover, in response to the question "whether the denial of Holy Communion to some Catholics in political life is necessary because of their public support for abortion on demand," the bishops did not endorse the policy of that small group of their membership who wanted such denial. "Given the wide range of circumstances involved in arriving at a prudent judgment on a matter of such seriousness, we recognize that such decisions rest with the individual bishop. . . . Bishops can legitimately make different judgments on the most prudent course of pastoral action."

I can think of only one way that bishops might earn a hearing for their teaching. While insisting on their convictions, they should refrain from questioning the integrity and good faith of those who disagree. Then they should become beacons of light on all issues concerning human life, the rights of women, and the rights of the poor and the oppressed.

Thus, while granting, for the sake of argument, that abortion is a more serious issue than the death penalty or preemptive war (or depriving workers of their pensions or health benefits or right to organize unions), bishops might imitate the Pope and more vigorously oppose the Iraq war and suggest that Catholic politicians who insist on the death penalty are not following the teachings of the Church. Cardinal Bernardin's "consistent ethic of life" theory might help bishops to look less like grand inquisitors fixated on one issue, however important, and more like men of graceful and generous concern for human life and dignity.

In the lead of a front-page article on the statement of the American Catholic bishops on abortion and politics, the *New York Times* asserted that the statement "leaves the door open for bishops to deny communion" to lawmakers who support abortion rights.

This lead fits the current media paradigm of bishops interfering in politics and in effect endorsing the policy of refusing the sacraments to Catholic politicians. Such an implication also indicates that the reporter is ignorant of the structure of the Catholic Church — and raises questions about her competence to report on it.

The collectivity of bishops has no power to enforce a decision on individual bishops. In fact, the bishop of Lincoln, Nebraska, refuses to cooperate with the requirements to report on sexual abuse in his diocese — unless the Pope orders him to do so. The door is always open for a bishop to deny the sacraments to anyone he wishes, and there is nothing that the rest of the bishops can do about it. If the bishop's decision violates canon law (and might very well do so), the victim's only recourse is an appeal to Rome. The bishops could not have closed the door if they had wanted to.

As the reporter should have known, the real issue was whether they would vote to make the denial of the sacraments their official policy. The *Times* article suggests that they did just that. Quite the contrary, the bishops did not endorse the policy of that small group of their membership who wanted to mandate the denial of Holy Communion to Catholics in political life who publicly supported abortion.

Such a decision is no surprise because the overwhelming majority of bishops have refrained from imitating those who are eager to engage in political action. If the *Times* had printed the text of their statement, its readers would have been able to decide for themselves what was said. The moderate tone of the statement indicates the dilemma Catholic leaders have found themselves in since *Roe v. Wade.* They believe, as they must, that a constitutional right to abortion is bad law. On the other hand, they know that most American women — including most Catholics — believe it is a right they should have, even if they do not intend to exercise it. Therefore, bishops are cast in the role of those who would take away the rights of women by the exercise of political clout. This is not a good position to be in when you avow, as they do in their statement, the need for "dialogue." But how do those who disagree with the Catholic Church engage in dialogue with religious leaders who believe that they are absolutely and clearly right and that others are absolutely and clearly wrong?

August 2004

The latest salvo in the Vatican's battle to reassert its teachings on sexuality and the family came late last month in the form of Cardinal Ratzinger's "Letter to the Bishops of the Catholic Church on the Collaboration of Men and Women in the Church and the World." To understand this letter, one must first comprehend how the German theological mind works. It finds an idea, elaborates the idea to its full logical implications, connects it to other ideas, and then refutes it. At no point is there any need to ask how many people share the idea or whether the connection with other ideas is anything more than an a priori linking of definitions.

Thus, after having asserted that the Church is expert in humanity (apparently even when it supported slavery), the cardinal says that radical feminism emphasizes the subordination of women, making it essential for women to seek power. This in turn leads to opposition between men and women, which has lethal effects on the structure of the family.

Secondly, he contends, radical feminism denies that the physical differences between men and women are important and hence equates homosexuality and heterosexuality and calls into question the family.

The German theological mind is content with such analysis. It does not ask how many feminists really hold these positions and how influential among women is the ideology that he has described. Harvard professor Mary Ann Glendon, president of the Pontifical Academy of Social Sciences and a frequent Vatican spokesperson, has said bluntly that few American women hold such ideas. But for a German theologian, it is the idea that matters.

Cardinal Ratzinger continues his letter with a description of the complementarity of men and women in the Scriptures and the Catholic tradition, a description that is useful and to which there can be no objection. However, by that time, the harm to the Church's image around the world has already been done. The Vatican once more asserts that it is against the rights of women.

It would have been most helpful if Cardinal Ratzinger had detailed at some length the abuses of women that gave rise not only to radical feminism but to the much more moderate feminism that most women in this country (and in Germany and Italy, too) support. He might have listed such abuses as rape, sexual slavery, incestuous abuse of daughters, granddaughters, and nieces, spousal abuse, sexual harassment in the workplace, sexual abuse by male coworkers, and discrimination in job promotion. All of these abuses happen in the "civilized" and "enlightened" Western World. In the rest of the world women are often little more than chattel, barely human, whose very lives are at the disposal of their men, and little girls can be sold into prostitution for tourists. Is Cardinal Ratzinger unaware of such activities? Does he realize that at least one-fifth of American women have been raped or targeted for rape? Does he think the rate would be any lower in Germany or Italy? Can he understand that some men, indeed many men, are truly the enemies of women? Has he ever stood in a golf course locker room and heard the demeaning and abusive conversation about women?

If the cardinal had devoted some attention, even minimal attention, to the historical and present abuse of women, his letter might have had a powerful impact on the whole world. It would have been a marvelous opportunity to preach moral and religious truth and to show that the Church was on the side of women.

I may have missed it, but I don't think any Episcopal conference anywhere in the world has condemned the epidemic abuse of women. Nor, as far as I know, has any American bishop written a pastoral letter on the subject. If priests preach on the subject, no one has reported it to me.

The pall of silence inside the Church on the subject of the abuse of women by husbands, fathers, military conquerors, ethnic cleansers, coworkers, strangers, and priests (who have even abused nuns in Africa) frightens me. I cannot understand why we are afraid of the subject. Are we covering up, just as we did on the abuse of children by priests? Do we feel guilty about it? Does it suit our purposes to deny in our own minds that it even exists? How could Cardinal Ratzinger not perceive it as a problem?

Many, many women, some of them exemplary Catholics, believe that the Church hates them. They think this not because they are radical feminists but because of the pious silence of the Church and its leaders.

I'm not sure that the conclave, whenever it happens, could possibly produce a Pope who would be inclined to write a document attacking the worldwide abuse of women. As I glance over the list of cardinals, I see no one likely to have the horrendous sins against women on his radar screen. No reason to be optimistic about the conclave's outcome on this or any other issue. As the Irish say, better the divil you know than the divil you don't know.

PART II

A statue atop the colonnade, at left, is seen as people fill St. Peter's Square after the announcement of the death of Pope John Paul II, Saturday, April 2, 2005. *(AP Photo/Alessandra Tarantino)*

A man waves the Polish flag in St. Peter's Square. John Paul II, the Polish Pontiff who led the Roman Catholic Church for more than a quarter century and became history's most-traveled Pope, has died at age eighty-four. *(AP Photo/Luca Bruno)*

Christoph Schönborn. Vienna student of Ratzinger. Inherited pedophile mess.
(AP Photo/Alessandra Tarantino)

Angelo Sodano. Papal Secretary of State. Possible "compromise" candidate.
(AP Photo/Andrew Medichini)

Francis Arinze. Roman Curia. Media favorite as possible African Pope. *(AP Photo/Shawn Baldwin)*

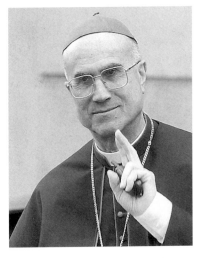

Tarcisio Bertone. Genoa. One-time assistant to Ratzinger. Announces soccer matches.
(AP Photo/Plinio Lepri)

Francis George. Chicago. "If an American could run, he would be *papabile*," says John Allen. *(AP Photo/Pier Paolo Cito)*

Cláudio Hummes. São Paulo, Brazil. "Not yet time for the third world."

(AP Photo/Alessandra Tarantino)

Carlo Maria Martini. Milan (Emeritus). Last liberal candidate. "I'm too old to be Pope." *(AP Photo/Pier Paolo Cito)*

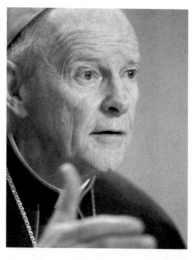

Theodore McCarrick. Archbishop of Washington. A smart, charming New York Irishman — and that's a compliment! *(AP Photo/Pier Paolo Cito)*

The faithful line up to reach St. Peter's Basilica at the Vatican, Tuesday, April 5, 2005, to say a personal farewell to the Pontiff.
(AP Photo/Peter Dejong)

Mourners queue to enter St. Peter's Basilica as the cardinals who will elect John Paul II's successor prepare for another round of meetings to arrange for the conclave.
(AP Photo/Peter Dejong)

Crowds pack St. Peter's Square at the Vatican, Friday, April 8, 2005, at the start of the funeral of Pope John Paul II.

(AP Photo/Gregorio Borgia)

Polish flags are waved in St. Peter's Square at the start of the funeral.

(AP Photo/Peter Dejong)

Royalty, political power brokers, and multitudes of the faithful pay their last respects to the Pope at a funeral promising to be one of the largest Western religious gatherings of modern times.
(*AP Photo/Lefteris Pitarakis*)

White smoke billows from the chimney of the Sistine Chapel at the Vatican, Tuesday, April 19, 2005, announcing that a Pope has been elected. (*AP Photo/Andrew Medichini*)

Cardinal Jorge Arturo Medina Estévez of Chile (Roman Curia) announces the *habemus papam* ("we have a Pope") from a balcony of St. Peter's Basilica. Joseph Ratzinger of Germany, who took the name of Pope Benedict XVI, is elected the 265th Pontiff of the Roman Catholic Church. *(AP Photo/Domenico Stinellis)*

Newly elected Pope Benedict XVI waves to the crowd from the central balcony of St. Peter's Basilica. *(AP Photo/Andrew Medichini)*

FEBRUARY 1, 2005

The Pope is in the Gemelli clinic with the flu and a sore throat. The death watch is on. How I hate it. I'm gearing up for the trip and the ordeal.

Among his other historic achievements, John Paul II was the first Pope to be treated in the hospital, when he was shot. There was no chance then to wonder whether it was reverent to take a Pope to a hospital.

It has been a great reign — but flawed, because no one listened to the laypeople or the lower clergy, through whom the Holy Spirit also speaks. The new Pope will have to heal many wounds. The Church is no more ideologically polarized than the United States is. But its leaders are. The laity and the lower clergy, the unpolarized people, are, however, far more to the left religiously than Americans are politically. They have pretty decisively rejected the authority of the leaders on certain matters. The new Pope will have to be pastoral, sensitive, prudent — and may well get torn apart. Some will want to see a return to the openness of the counciliar years, others will want a white terror — a cracking down on everyone who disagrees. Grim days ahead.

FEBRUARY 25, 2005

The Pope is out of the hospital but is obviously very sick. The end is near, and I feel sad. None of us should have to die.

I have pondered the present situation in the Church often and read John Allen's recent dispatches from Rome carefully, and I can only conclude that the people over there have no idea what's happening. They're playing music on the *Titanic*. The Church is back in the Middle Ages — formless, inchoate, disorganized. No one listens to anyone anymore. The Archbishop of Denver, who led the big campaign to deny Senator John Kerry Communion, received exactly six votes for office (out of more than two hundred) at the bishops' meeting — which shows that even among his own he has no support.

The basic beliefs of the people are still there — in helping the poor, receiving the Eucharist, God in the Sacraments, reverence for Our Lady — yet somehow the powers that be are wringing their hands in near despair that the faith is being destroyed.

The institutional Catholic Church is in deep trouble. The more immediate problems are the sex abuse scandal — which has not gone away and won't for a long time — and the clumsy efforts of some U.S. bishops to deliver votes for the Republican Party. There are three chronic problems in the Catholic Church to which it is not even trying to respond — the decline in Mass attendance, the decline in vocations, and the decline in parochial school attendance.

Ask what is causing the problems and you'll hear personal opinions and clichés, most of which blame the laity. They're materialist, consumerist, secularist, weak in faith, caught in the grip of American hypersexual culture, etc., etc. Having delivered themselves of that wisdom — which cannot be verified because it cannot admit of falsification — the priests who prate such nonsense settle back complacently. There is nothing for them to do except turn on the TV.

It is difficult to imagine that another large institution faced with similar difficulties would be satisfied with such easy and self-serving analysis, much less adopt demoralizing policies in response to the apparent bad news. The Church closes parishes because people are not attending Mass, closes seminaries because there are no more vocations, and closes schools because apparently no one wants them or needs them anymore. No hope, no leadership, no vision. Bad news, clichéd judgments, and then cut and run! Pessimism and despair carry the day. Real bright!

My research shows that Catholic priests are the happiest men in America and that Catholic schools are among the best educational bargains. Catholic art and liturgy are the richest devotional heritage in the Western world. Yet let's close up shop and run for the hills without trying to figure out why we have troubles.

We do studies of Catholic schools, of course, and expensive studies at that, but their purpose is to figure out which schools to close, not to ask why some schools are closing and others have waiting lists. Priests write petitions to Rome advocating the abolition of celibacy, but they never ask themselves any serious questions about the quality of preaching and liturgy in their parishes. Nor do they ask themselves when was the last time they tried to recruit young men into the priesthood.

A cardinal back in the forties said to an expert who suggested routine research (presumably something more sophisticated than counting noses on an October Sunday), "The Catholic Church doesn't need research, sir. We have the Holy Spirit." No one quite says that anymore, but the presumption is the same — guesswork, strongly held opinions, faith in God, and panic when the money seems to be running low. That will have to serve for what in the secular world is called "R and D."

God help us all, though we don't deserve God's help if we're not willing to do anything ourselves.

I have my own opinions on these matters — homilies and liturgies are bad, no one recruits, no one promotes the schools. Unlike the opinions of some other priests, these can be disproved by research, if the Church would devote the resources to it. "The sexual revolution" or "secularism" or "consumerism" are explanations that cannot be falsified and so cannot be proved, either. If you're a priest or even a bishop, you make major decisions by wetting your finger and putting it in the air or reading the entrails of dead fowl or guessing or talking to your stockbroker.

I argue for research not because I intend to do it anymore (my name on a research project causes priests to reject a priori the findings), but because I cannot imagine the CEO of any other institution operating without it. We've been around a long time and so we'll muddle through, our leaders think, even if that is another form of *tentatio Dei* — tempting God.

It may not be possible to turn off the Catholic laity. If sexual abuse, bankruptcy, and political meddling didn't do it, what will? Maybe closing their schools and churches without good reason — or because our financial people say that land is ripe for resale — will do it.

My longtime colleague William C. McCready once said to me, "The Catholic Church is in terrible trouble." I nodded. He went on, "All it has left are the Catholic schools and the Blessed Mother, and a lot of you guys don't believe in either anymore."

MARCH 20, 2005

He's back in the hospital, poor dear man. A "relapse" of the flu. They've done a trach. My guess is pneumonia. The phone is ringing off the hook again. Media vultures. What do I know that they don't know?

I am grimly pessimistic about the whole business of the conclave. I can't imagine the present crowd doing anything except making a bad situation worse.

So much depends on the mood of the electors when they arrive. I hope they realize how serious is the need for change. I suspect, however, that they'll want to tighten things up.

I should clarify some misconceptions about papal elections.

1. Papal elections are different from other elections because the Holy Spirit takes a direct hand in the outcome. Oh? Is God's Spirit therefore responsible for the outcome of the Renaissance conclaves, which were mostly simoniacal (bought and sold)? Was she behind the conclave that produced Rodrigo Borgia (Alexander VI), in which only five of the twenty-one cardinals had not been bought? Was she responsible for the deals made in the latrines before the election of Pius II? Was she responsible for the elections of the tenth century when the women of important Roman families had de facto control of the outcome of the elections? Was the Holy Spirit responsible for the election of Stephen VI, who dragged the body of his predecessor out of the tomb, put him on trial in pontifical vestments, then mutilated his body and threw it into the Tiber? Can we blame the Spirit for the election of John XII (at the age of eighteen), who would die of a stroke in bed with a married woman?

Or did the Holy Spirit change her mind when, after choosing Clement XIV (one of the weakest Popes in history), who promised to suppress the Jesuits, she chose Pius VII, who unsuppressed them?

Even Cardinal Ratzinger has argued that God is not responsible for a specific outcome.

In truth, the election of a Pope is like all other elections, a very human event with very human participants and very human concerns and ambitions. To deny this is to deny the humanity of the Church. Not to put too fine an edge on things, a papal election is politics. The important question is whether the politics of a conclave are intelligent politics or stupid politics, honest politics or, as they have often been in the past, incredibly hypocritical and corrupt politics. The Spirit is involved in all human events, but often because of human malice and ignorance, she is not able to accomplish her preferred scenario.

2. Saintly men make the best Popes.   Not necessarily so. Ideally, the Pope should be devout. But sanctity does not guarantee administrative ability or political skills. San Celestino was a very holy man who knew he had no abilities and quickly resigned. Pius V may have been too quick to excommunicate the English monarch Elizabeth I and supported some of the cruelties of the Roman Inquisition. Saint Pius X did grave harm to the Church with his exaggerated and unnecessarily sweeping condemnation of Modernism.

3. Popes have always been celibate.   We know that Peter had a mother-in-law, so he must have had a wife. Pious Catholic legend insists that his wife had died, but there's no evidence of this. Since celibacy was not expected of bishops in the earliest days (one of Saint Paul's epistles insists that bishops should have only one wife), it is probable that at least several of the early Popes were married men. Innocent I (401) was the son of a Pope — Anastasius I, whom he succeeded. Several later Popes were also sons of Popes. Moreover, the Popes of the tenth century frequently had mistresses, including Sergius III, John X, and John XI. Alexander VI fathered two children while he was Pope (his mistress being sixteen-year-old Giulia Farnese, "Giulia la Bella").

During the eighteenth and nineteenth centuries, Popes were often products of the administrative service of the Papal States. It was customary for younger men in the bureaucracy to take minor orders and on occasion mistresses. If their careers prospered, they would later seek priestly ordination and give up the mistress. Some Popes of that era were alleged to have followed that career path and even to have made their sons cardinals. Since there is no solid documentation of these charges, there is no point in mentioning their names.

There is in fact nothing in the essential nature of the Church to prevent a married man from being elected Pope and continuing to live with his wife. Rules and laws would have to be changed, dispensations would have to be granted, but all this would theoretically be possible. Whether it would be desirable is another matter. In any case, it is not likely to happen in the immediate future — or for a long time.

4. There have been many great Popes.   History has granted the title to only two men — Leo I (440–461) and Gregory I (590–604), both of whom incidentally insisted that bishops ought to be elected by clergy and laypeople, including the Bishop of Rome. Will any Popes of the twentieth and present century be considered "great"? John XXIII? John Paul II? It depends on who writes the history books.

MARCH 23, 2005 (WEDNESDAY OF HOLY WEEK)

Rumors from Rome have the Pope not recovering as quickly as they had hoped. His doctors are not making statements. On the other hand, he did wave from the window of his apartment today — but did not, according to the reports, appear particularly healthy. Many have questioned why he doesn't resign. The answer I give is that he's the Pope and he doesn't want to resign. That would, in his perspective, be false to his duty. Is that self-serving? I don't know. I'm sure that many around him are subtly encouraging him to stay the course, lest they lose their jobs or at least their power. How long can this go on? I'm inclined to think that it can go on for a long time.

John Allen has an interesting summary in his weekly report from Rome:

> Inside the Vatican, there are naturally different views about what to make of recent events.

Vatican personnel are unanimous in the conviction that John Paul II has been a historically important pope, and that his determination to fulfill the mission God has given him is a powerful spiritual witness. At the same time, some have long harbored doubts about what they see as the (potentially inadvertent) personalization of the papacy under John Paul — his pop-star status, his travels, his grand events in St. Peter's Square, the very personal nature of some of his canonizations and beatifications, the way his personal spiritual tastes (such as the Divine Mercy devotion associated with Polish St. Faustina Kowalska) have been elevated as normative, and the way the pope pronounces on so many matters, risking confusion between personal commentary and magisterial teaching.

Strong words, and I think absolutely correct. John is not the sort of reporter who would make up such mutterings. I wonder, however, how much that kind of thought will affect the conclave.

MARCH 24, 2005 (HOLY THURSDAY)

After the conclave, what about Europe?

What is the Catholic Church to do? Indeed, what are all Christian Churches to do about Europe? With the exception of a very few countries, religion seems moribund in Europe. The question is being asked urgently as the time for a conclave once again seems near. There are three basic orientations among

Catholic leaders on the subject of Europe — orientations that reveal both a theology of the Church and a theology of the world.

The first might be called the "steadfast" Church. It says that religious faith is practically dead in Europe. The Church ought not to compromise its teachings to accommodate people who are for all practical purposes a lost cause. Consumerism, paganism, materialism, and secularism now rule in Western Europe and are spreading to Eastern Europe. The Church, for its part, has the Truth and must preach the Truth without any variation in its language, its style, its method. Eventually the truth of Catholicism will become evident and there may be the beginnings of a religious revival in this pagan subcontinent — but on our terms. Not quite so sharply stated, perhaps, this is the policy of the present papacy. One calls on Europe to return home without expecting it to listen.

The second orientation could be called the "engaged" Church. Archbishop Diarmuid (Dermot) Martin of Dublin recently called upon his priests to create a "humble, listening Church." Cardinal Hummes of São Paulo, in a recent commentary on the Vatican II document *Gaudium et Spes* (Joy and Hope), called for a servant church and one that was always in dialogue with all religions. A humble, listening, servant church, constantly in dialogue? Those words are left over from the conciliar era but have lost most of their excitement and meaning. If the cardinal and the archbishop really want that kind of Church, there's a lot of work to be done. The Irish clergy and hierarchy will have to go a long way before they adopt a modality of humility and listening. Ditto for the Americans. In fact, it is almost hilariously funny to think of most of the leaders in either country being capable of either humility or listening.

John Allen has recently added a third group — the "disengaged" Church, one that simply gives up on Europe as beyond redemption.

Two sociological facts are pertinent to this discussion. First, as my Arizona colleague Mark Chaves has argued, secularization does not mean that people are any less religious but only that institutional churches have lost much of their control over their people and society. For weal or woe, an educated population will not accept Church teaching as a matter for blind obedience. Maybe the churches should have opposed the education of their laity. It would be a lot easier for bishops and priests if they were still dealing with peasants.

Second, my own recent research shows that in most European countries, belief in life after death has increased sharply among the cohorts born since 1945. While the younger cohorts may not attend church all that often, they are still believers of a sort. Condemning them or repeating all the old rules to them will have no influence.

The advantage of the "steadfast" or the "disengaged" Church is that there is no particular need to change or to work or even to listen. Self-righteous certainty carries the day.

I don't see how the "engaged" Church has a chance at the conclave, whenever it may be. While many churchmen may secretly be unhappy with the present posture of the "steadfast" or "disengaged" Church, they are hardly numerous enough or well organized enough to choose a candidate who views the world through the eyes of the "engaged" Church and then elect him Pope. The Vatican Council is too far in the past and has been too vitiated of its true meaning for that to be possible. The next Pope will doubtless echo the sentiments of the present Vatican — that all hope for Europe was lost when it left religion out of the new EU constitution.

MARCH 27, 2005 (EASTER SUNDAY)

The media are playing up the Pope's nonparticipation in the Holy Week services as though it is a matter of great surprise and dismay, something almost impossible. As usual they miss the point. He's a sick man. No one denies that. He has lost the power of speech. No one denies that. He's not going to quit, but the subtext of many media stories is that he should quit. Those around him, one has to suppose, support his resolve in part because while he lives, they keep their jobs. An Italian journalist, with the characteristic flair for the dramatic that leads Italian journalists often to go beyond the truth, argues that the Vatican is now trying something new and original — running the papacy by television images. The implication is that behind these images a cabal of men will actually dominate decisions. Anyone who knows anything about the history of this papacy understands that's the way it's been all along. The Pope has been in charge of day-to-day decisions only from a great distance. The images assure the crowds that come to Rome and those watching from around the world that we still have a Pope, albeit a sick and dying Pope. Again, that is not intended to deceive anyone and probably does not.

The Pope's involvement in this terrible Terry Schiavo case is, it seems to me, unfortunate. The issue is whether a feeding tube is an extraordinary means to preserve life in someone whose brain cortex is no longer functioning.

Many, perhaps most, Catholic moralists tend to think that it is an extraordinary means. The Pope disagrees, which looks like a change of practice if not of doctrine. Everyone — i.e., curialists, bishops, right-to-life laity and clergy — is taking a stand on the case in line with what the Pope has said, though it is generally thought that while he was being authoritative, he was not being definitive.

I am inclined to think that the Pope would have been better advised not to intrude in the discussion among the moral theologians. As I remarked earlier, he seems to have the tendency to identify Church teaching with his own opinions, which might not be such a good thing.

March 28, 2005

The Pope did not bless the Easter Monday crowds today. Bad weather was given as the reason. We're in the final days, I think. I dread the trip to Rome.

Friday, April 1, 2005

The Pope is dying — urinary infection, falling blood pressure, aging body just falling apart. I remember the day of the first papal mass in the Piazza, when he waved the papal crosier almost as if it were a battle-ax, a sign of victory. He looked so young and vigorous and healthy. A sign to all of us of how limited our lives are at best.

The media are buzzing around like vultures. I'm at Grand Beach, where I was when Paul VI died. Then I was sad but excited. Now I feel worn and depressed. So much has gone wrong in the Church during the last twenty-seven years, so many dreams blighted.

I'm busy worrying about flight reservations, my clothes and small computer in a trunk coming from Arizona. I wish everything could be bracketed until after the funeral. It all seems indecent now.

My third and last conclave. I don't quite have the energy that I had for the last two. Still, it's a great event — though, as I have often said, not a good way to elect the leader of a billion or so people.

12:54:27 PM

Septic shock, they say now, failing kidneys, shallow breathing. He probably won't last the night.

I should be there. Why didn't I realize that I should be there?

Uncanny pictures on TV. The Piazza, filled with people, is illumined by floodlights. It's like the night John Paul II was elected: a pleasant night, crowds of people praying in the baroque environment.

I remember the first conclave I watched on the black-and-white TV in Christ the King Rectory. "Annunciabo Vobis gaudium magnum, Habemus papam, Angelo Cardinalis Sanctae Romanae Ecclesiase Roncalli qui sibi imposuit nomen Johanes!"

Cheers from the crowd, who, like the rest of us, didn't know who this new Pope John was. Seventy-seven years old, Irving R. Levine said on TV, patriarch of Venice. What the heck! Then this fat man with the funny face came out and gave his first blessing *urbi et orbi.* Strong, firm, determined voice — a hint of the world of change that would later sweep the Church. I hope, I thought then, that someday I'll be at a conclave.

The bloom is off the rose. The hope of those years has faded. Yet it is still great theater, Catholic theater, and my heart breaks not only for the poor Pope but for the Church, for all that was lost. God will have to surprise us.

Despite my reservations, I'm still caught in the dreams of almost fifty years ago. I need to be there.

SATURDAY, APRIL 2, 2005

The Pope is dead. I have a hard time thinking straight. The Church is not doing a good job these days, and the idiot commentary on TV only makes things worse. I went through a list of the cardinals this afternoon. There's no way we can get what the Church needs out of that crowd.

Like I say, the Holy Spirit has a lot of work to do.

The late Pope was a scholar, a poet, a charismatic presence, a brave and holy man — he was surely one of the most influential religious leaders in the world. His stand against war, most specifically the Iraq war, presented a vigorous and determined challenge to conservative American Catholics — which most of them simply ignored. He stood for what the late Cardinal Bernardin called the consistent ethic of life. He condemned abortion, war, and the death penalty.

One can proclaim his greatness and influence, praise his determination in the face of death, and celebrate his long reign, and still raise questions about his legacy. The Catholic Church today is polarized by deep disagreements between progressives and those who would restore the status quo ante the Vatican Council; between laity and lower clergy on the one hand and the Roman Curia on the other; between those who favor the decentralization suggested by the council's theory of "collegiality" and those who favor ever tighter control from Rome. The next Pope, who may well be chosen because he is seen as a "healer," will have a very difficult time and will risk being torn apart by the centrifugal energies in the Church.

John Paul inherited a Church in deep confusion after the appealing Pope John and the hesitant Pope Paul. When he came to office in 1978, he determined to end the chaos definitively. His style of Church rule was the one he knew from his native Poland and which the whole Church had practiced since the French Revolution. He sought to restore order and discipline by laying down the rules and demanding that the laity and clergy accept his right and authority to do so.

It was already too late in the day to implement such a strategy. Unquestioning obedience was no longer an automatic response and had not been since 1968. The laity and the lower clergy had already decided that in the area of human sexuality, the Church no longer had the right to order them. In retrospect, a sensitive strategy of patience, openness, and consultation might have been much more effective. However, the Pope by personality and life history seems to have been incapable of governing that way. Alienation between the Vatican and much of the membership of the Church has increased, made worse each time a seemingly arbitrary edict appeared from the Vatican.

The extremely conservative bishops John Paul appointed, usually on curial recommendation, further offended many of the laity and the lower clergy. He rarely engaged in serious consultation with the bishops of the world and listened only to the laity that he knew agreed with him. This, one had to assume, was the way he thought the papacy ought to govern the Church.

The Catholic Church, so attractive during the time of Pope John, lost much of its respect and esteem — especially because it was perceived, perhaps unfairly, to be hostile to both women and homosexuals.

To make matters worse, the sexual abuse crisis — which the Vatican still would like to pretend is an American problem — has spread throughout Europe and has compromised the credibility of the Church leadership. The Pope's reaction to it seemed to many to be less vigorous than was appropriate. Sex was the touchstone of his restoration of order to the Church, but not, it might have been fairly said, the sexual behavior of priests.

No one in their right mind would question the personal virtue, the good intentions, the sincerity of the late Pontiff. Yet clearly he failed to restore the discipline of the Church's traditional sexual ethic. The lower clergy and the laity are even less likely today, despite all his efforts, to accept that discipline than when he came to office.

The most important decision the next Pope must make is whether it is time for a change in the papacy's style of governance.

SUNDAY, APRIL 3, 2005

The late Father Walter Imbiorski, a man with family roots deep in Chicago's ethnic politics, once remarked that "Dick Daley could wire a conclave in forty-eight hours."

"That long?" I replied in feigned surprise.

He meant the first Mayor Daley. Not that the current Mayor Daley couldn't figure out the politics of a conclave that quickly. The conclave, you see, is a political event, arguably the political event par excellence.

Some will think such a comment approaches blasphemy. In fact, according to Aristotle (who ought to know!), politics, the art of governing, is the second most honorable art, ranking only after poetry. Politicians are masters of the art not of the perfect but of the possible, of supporting not the best possible candidate but the candidate who can win, the candidate of the broadest possible coalition rather than the most admirable.

Conclaves are much like American political conventions in the old days (as depicted brilliantly by the late Steve Neal in his book *Happy Days Are Here Again*), though in the case of a conclave, all the campaigning is done indirectly, behind the scenes, by subtle hints and conversations, winks, slight nods of the head, and pregnant silences, which are typical of both the Roman style and the Irish smoke-filled room.

The cardinals have the advantage that they can proceed in secrecy and the disadvantage that they are less likely to be familiar with the candidates. No one runs openly for the papacy — not anymore, anyway. Moreover, with some possible exceptions, none of the cardinals wants to be Pope. They all know what an excruciatingly difficult job it is. On the other hand, there are some who know they're under consideration — as John Paul II did when he came to the conclave in 1978 with an electrocardiogram in his briefcase. Few would turn down what they would consider God's will.

Such men are frequently invited to speak around the world so that others can have some sort of idea what kind of Pope they would make. They accept these invitations with considerable ambivalence, but they accept them. Thus Cardinal Cláudio Hummes, the Brazilian Franciscan (of German ancestry), recently gave a powerful presentation in Rome on an "open, servant Church." The electors have a pretty good idea of what kind of Pope he would be.

As they arrive in Rome and view the body of Pope John Paul, the cardinals will be discreet in their brief conversations with one another. They will speak in general terms about what the Church needs. Then, as they settle into their residences, they will have more specific conversations with those who share the same residence (many American cardinals stay in the North American College up on the Janiculum Hill overlooking St. Peter's) or those whom they might see at lunch or supper.

After the Pope's funeral, while the "General Congregations" (formal meetings) are going on, the cardinals will hear talks by some of their number whom the Curia wants them to hear. But after the meetings adjourn, the "consultations" will become more intense and odds-on candidates will take shape. As in the Cook County Democratic organization, some of the "committeemen" are clueless and some very sophisticated. Counting votes is much more difficult before the conclave because no one is expected to make a hard and fast commitment (though, like political bosses, some cardinals have very long memories).

In the conclave itself, there are a couple of ballots in which complimentary votes are cast for friends ("favorite sons"), and then the electors settle down to business. At this point several (usually two) different scenarios can emerge. A consensus candidate might be elected — as in the case of John Paul I, the only electable Italian who could stand between the two most powerful men, Cardinal Siri of Genoa and Cardinal Benelli of Florence. When the poor September Pope died, the supporters of these two men deadlocked and the conclave had to turn to a compromise candidate — John Paul II. Pius XII in the 1930s was a consensus candidate, as was Paul VI in the 1960s. Both men were widely considered well qualified (though some Italians, including Cardinal Siri, made Paul's election less than unanimous).

John XXIII was a compromise between two similar factions, a nice old man who would appoint new cardinals for another election and not stir things up. That election proved a rule that also applies in American politics. You never know how a winner might behave.

Who will be the winner this time?

Handicapping a papal election is a risky business. If all horse players die broke, all those who think they can predict the outcome of a conclave may have to spend the rest of their lives explaining why they were wrong. Yet predictions must be essayed if only to have an answer to the question everyone asks. Two issues seem to be on everyone's mind these days — age and geography.

For most of Catholic history, before the advent of modern medicine, the average term on the throne of the fisherman (who, by the way, never had a throne!) was five years. Many churchmen believe that long papacies are not a good idea — though it might be politically incorrect to say that after the second longest has come to an end.

Nonetheless, age will be very much on the minds of many of the electors. A candidate over sixty-five or even over seventy might have, all other things being equal, a better chance than a younger man.

Moreover, there is a certain sense that, after electing a Pope from what was then the second world, it might now be time to elect a third-world bishop, one from either Africa or South America. So some of the speculation one hears and reads begins with likely candidates from the third world.

I'm not sure whether the Europeans — especially the Italians — and the North Americans are willing to buy into such a politically correct scheme. On the other hand, a presentable South American Pope would be a major image victory for the Church and generate a sense of a brave new beginning, much like the election of the first Polish Pope.

Latin American cardinals have left little doubt that they believe the huge number of Catholics in Latin America almost entitles them to their turn in the papacy. However, there are only twenty-one Latin American cardinals and eleven more from Africa, hardly enough to influence the outcome of the conclave unless the Europeans with their fifty-one votes swing that way.

Several Latin Americans are mentioned — Cláudio Hummes of Brazil, Darío Castrillón Hoyos from Colombia, and Oscar Rodríguez Maradiaga of Honduras. The first two are seventy and seventy-five respectively; the latter is sixty-two. All of them would be less than enthusiastic about America, capitalism, and globalization. The latter two attacked America at the time of the sexual abuse crisis, Cardinal Rodríguez blaming the Jewish media for the crisis. American reaction to the election of a new Pope would not make many cardinals hesitate. However, Cardinal Hummes — a Franciscan of German ancestry and a supporter of Brazilian president Lula da Silva — might be more acceptable to the Europeans anyway. Cardinal Francis Arinze (seventy-two) of Nigeria generates a lot of media attention but apparently not much enthusiasm among fellow cardinals.

On the other hand, it is alleged that Italians feel it is time for another Italian papacy. Dionigi Tettamanzi (seventy-one) is supposed to look like Pope John, to be affable and friendly to everyone, and to be superb on television. He is also close to the conservative Catholic organization Opus Dei. Cardinal Giovanni Battista Re (seventy-one) is a skilled and pragmatic administrator and diplomat and also allegedly quite charming, though many of his recent appointments as head of the congregation for making bishops have been disappointing. From the American point of view, he gave immediate support to the drastic response of the American hierarchy to the sexual abuse problem. Cardinal Angelo Scola (sixty-three) is supposed to be a brilliant theologian and quite conservative.

Other Europeans are mentioned. Walter Kasper (seventy-two), a German theologian and ecumenist; Godfried Danneels (seventy-one), a gifted and perceptive Belgian and a strong supporter of more decentralized authority in the Church; and Christoph Schönborn (sixty) of Vienna, a very conservative theologian and an Austrian aristocrat. The first two are probably too "progressive" for the electors, and Schönborn has not been completely successful in Vienna and is perhaps too young. Miroslav

Vlk (seventy-two) of Prague might be a dark horse among those who want to keep the papacy in Eastern Europe.

The current cardinals' average age is about seventy-two. Only a few have served as parish priests. One-third made their careers in the Curia at the diocese level. Another group of about thirty are from the office of the Vatican Secretary of State, Vatican congregations, or other Vatican offices.

Taking into account age and geography, I could imagine a contest between Hummes (if the Latin Americans are able to get their act together) and Tettamanzi (or Re as a last-minute Italian choice), with the balance of power held by the northern Europeans (if they are able to get their act together). The conclave, I predict, crawling out on a bigger limb, will last no more than three days.

And the winner?

Right now a German Brazilian Franciscan looks like a pretty good one-person balanced ticket.

Monday, April 4, 2005

As the conclave draws near (and I wait in desperation for my clothes and computer from Tucson), the billion or so Catholic laypeople will watch with varying degrees of interest. Some will find the process either archaic or boring. Others will watch with mild interest when the white smoke rises above the Sistine Chapel. Still others will be deeply concerned about the outcome — either because it will confirm that the Second Vatican Council has been relegated to the trash can of history or because it will show that the spirit of the council may still be alive.

For a thousand years and more, the Church was a democracy in the selection of leaders. A democratic ethos, perverted and corrupted, pervades the election of the Pope by the College of Cardinals. Theoretically, they are the parish priests of Rome come together to elect their bishop just as every diocese elected its own bishop in those first thousand years. There is unfortunately not even a symbolic nod of the head to the equally ancient custom that the people of Rome had to consent to the election of their bishop. Popes Leo the Great and Gregory the Great, who laid down the law that the one who presides over all should be chosen by all, would be shocked and indeed scandalized at the oligarchic and secret sessions in the Sistine Chapel. Doubtless at that point in the future when democracy is restored to the Church (which, after all, brought democracy to the Western world), historians will marvel at the patent abuse that this conclave and the many others before it represented. They will perhaps blame the conclave system (along with the temporal rule of the Pope) for most of the problems the Church experienced during the second millennium.

On American Airlines Flight 110
Wednesday, April 6, 2005

There seems to be a certain nastiness emerging as a result of the television coverage of the Pope's death and now the wake and funeral. Some Catholic writers are writing about the limitations of John Paul II's administration — the rigidity, the centralization, the authoritarianism, and, as some call it, his "hatred" of women. Two women stopped me yesterday on the streets of

Chicago to say, "Well, he was a good man, but he hated women."
I don't think he hated women. I think he liked women, indeed
more so than some previous Popes. But he certainly wasn't especially enlightened on the subject. He said women could not be
priests because the Church did not have the power from Jesus to
make them priests. He said this position was held by all the bishops of the world, but he never did consult all the bishops of the
world about the issue. Women are unforgiving about it, and I
don't blame them. It was a black mark on his administration, and
the Church is going to have to pay for it in years to come. John
Cahill had a piece on the *New York Times* Op-Ed page with
some criticisms of the Pope, and the letters column today really
beat up on him. The conservatives who have made John Paul
their own, leaving out issues like war and the death penalty, will
tolerate no criticism of him. I thought Cahill's remarks were well
within the limits of good taste when someone's body is not yet in
the ground, or in the basement of St. Peter's, as the case may be.
But there will be nastiness between the conservatives and the
liberals in the years to come, months to come anyway, no matter
who is elected Pope.

Already, some cardinals are saying we ought not to have a
South American. An American cardinal said on television last
night, "John Paul was a good Pope, not because he was from
Poland, but because he was a man of faith; not because he was a
good actor, but because he was a man of faith." Well, that's certainly true. But it could imply for the South Americans that
somehow they don't have any men of similar faith who could be
Pope. What the cardinals seem to forget is that the Pope's being
Polish was a big help. And his acting ability was a big help. Indeed, what the American cardinal should have said was that, all

other things being equal, it might be better to have a Pope from a third-world country. I don't know why he didn't choose to say that. I suspect he really believes that to be true, but he had to lecture us about what is required of a Pope. Faith: yes; competence: yes — and those things assured, we look for other qualities. There are a billion Catholics in the world, as everybody is saying, but Brazil has about 200 million (maybe a little less because of the Evangelicals, but let's round it off at 200 million). That's 20 percent of all the Catholics in the world in one huge South American country. And if there's a man of talent and ability from there, so much the better that he be made Pope. Also, it might be a good change to have a Pope who views the world in a very different light from the Europeans or North Americans.

I wonder how the cardinal electors are reacting to the swarms of people coming to Rome to pay tribute to the Pope. What I fear is that they will draw an easy conclusion: the people worship this Pope because of the strong moral stands he's taken and because of his authoritative style, and they want another Pope just like him. However, the people who come to view the Pope's body and to attend the funeral are not necessarily typical; they are not necessarily a good sample. More to the point, who knows what they really want? Are they here to endorse the policies of John Paul or are they in Rome to celebrate the man? It is not clear, and in fact there is little reason to believe, that the crowds swarming to Rome and the enormous worldwide attention are a confirmation of the rigidity and authoritarianism that often marked John Paul's papacy.

On the other hand, the cardinal electors might be scared stiff by the so-called rock-star pop-culture demonstration here in Rome, and may feel either that they have to elect another man just like John Paul II, which would be very hard to find, or that they must elect someone very different so that the emphasis will be on a man of faith and not on personal charisma.

One cannot discount the charisma. John Paul was a man of enormous physical and psychological presence. He trained as an actor and probably had innate theatrical ability. He created a powerful public image and presence. Once his face appeared on television, he demanded everybody's attention. And his life and death confirmed that. To say that he is getting rock-star attention is merely to say that he was a well-known popular figure, even to those who disagreed with him.

He was also certainly a good and holy man, no doubt better and more holy than I am. He was more liberal on social and peace matters — immigration, Iraq, the death penalty, obligation to poor countries — than most American Catholics. When you combine the personal virtue with the public charisma, he was an enormous figure. The Church can't expect someone like that every time around; it can't expect it more than once or twice in a millennium. So the cardinal electors have a problem. They can't ignore the charisma of John Paul, but neither can they translate it into a theological endorsement of centralization and authoritarianism.

They must realize that John Paul's charisma shaped the papacy and is going to lead to expectations for the future. An unhappy Pope, a nervous Pope, a frowning Pope, an irritable Pope, won't play anymore. When I think of the way some of the Roman cardinals treat questions at a press conference, I'm just dismayed. They have learned nothing. The next Pope can't be inarticulate, irritable, or authoritarian in his personal tone because he won't have John Paul's charisma to cover for that. And he apparently should speak many languages. Tettamanzi, one of the leading Italian candidates, can speak only Italian. Hummes, from Brazil, can certainly speak Portuguese. He can understand English, I'm told, but doesn't speak it very well. Presumably he knows Italian if he's a cardinal.

The public persona of the Pope, in summary, is far more important now than it ever was before, and the Church is going to have to live with that. And if the cardinal electors don't keep that in mind, they'll have a disaster on their hands. There's a nice irony in that the Pope certainly was a telegenic personality for the late twentieth and early twenty-first centuries, but the Church as such has little skill and in fact little interest in learning the skills of public presentation. Cardinals, by and large, are not good in front of a television camera. They're constrained by too many obligations, too many people to keep happy. They don't seem to be relaxed or confident. It's unfortunate indeed. We haven't caught on to television, the Internet, and globalized culture.

The question that seems to fascinate many of the journalists in Rome (and in America) is: How could so many Catholics adore John Paul II and yet ignore the things he taught? I suspect the answer is that these people distinguish not with any serious reflection but intuitively and distinctively between the symbolic value of the Pope and what the Pope teaches. They cheer the first and don't hear the second because they don't want to hear it. They adore the singer and don't hear the song. If they couldn't hear it from John Paul II, how are they going to hear it from anybody else?

That may be one of the most striking phenomena about the late Pope. His persona, his presence, his charisma, held the

Church together despite all the stresses and strains, although he reinforced positions that people don't accept, don't want to accept, don't believe they have to accept, and are never going to accept again. Catholics the world over, according to our data, don't accept the Church's sexual ethic. It doesn't mean they're complete pagans, that they're materialists or secularists or all the other labels Catholics love around here, but it does mean they reserve the right to make their own decisions about sexuality. This is an enormous problem for the Church.

Mike Hout suggested to me some time ago that when Catholic people cheer for the Pope, they're cheering for themselves. This sounds strange until one realizes that the Pope is a sacrament of the Church, the Pope stands for the Church, the Pope reveals the Church. And laypeople are the Church. Or, to put it in a little less complicated fashion: because Catholics are a sacramental community, a community in which the symbols and signs are extremely important, the personality of the Pope is something you can cheer enthusiastically because you're cheering for what he represents. That is the long Catholic tradition. But you're not necessarily cheering for his particular interpretations of the tradition. If you're inside the Church, Mike's theory is easy enough to comprehend. If you're outside, it makes no sense at all. How can you adore, worship, demonstrate for, flock to the wake of your religious leader if on certain fundamental issues you do not agree with him? In part, of course, it's because of the man the Pope was.

The successor can't possibly be the same kind of man. But how will he deal with the laity's perceived right to make their own decisions (particularly on matters of sexuality)? Do the electors understand the tensions that exist among the faithful and among the clergy, too? Have they deceived themselves into thinking that there are no serious problems? Have they taken the absurd position that if you're just tough enough and resolute enough you can overcome the laity's resistance, or simply dismiss the laity as not important?

They forget that the Holy Spirit speaks through the laypeople as well as through the College of Cardinals. They don't know what's going on among the laypeople — especially in their married lives. They don't comprehend the enormous change that has come from a demographic revolution where marriages last on average fifty years instead of twelve years. This transformation of human sexual union creates many spiritual problems that I don't think even the parish clergy understand, to say nothing of the bishops and the cardinals and the Popes. The things they say about sex and marriage, save for the Pope's early audience talks on sex (which were brilliant though obscure), simply do not impinge on the consciousness of most of the electors. They tell you that they know what's going on with the laity — and they're convinced that they do know, but of course they don't. In this respect, the problem of upward communication that I mentioned earlier in the book is most serious and most intense. Even many parish priests don't know what's going on in the heads of their parishioners. The upward communication is weak at that level, so how much more serious it is at a level of parish priests and bishops or bishops and the Pope. The men going into conclave on the eighteenth of April are going to be steering the ship, the bark of Peter as we love to call it, in a thick fog without a map and without radar.

One of the nice things about the trip to Rome for the conclave is learning from *Time* magazine that Jordan Bonfante has been called out of semiretirement to come back to Rome to cover the conclave. An extraordinarily intelligent thing for *Time* to do! I'm surprised there's enough collective memory at that place to realize what kind of a journalist Jordan is and how good a job he did twenty-seven years ago.

On the plane on the way over I have time to reflect on the last conclaves — in 1978. I left for Rome so quickly after Pope Paul's death that I was there for the wake. I went up to the Sala Clementina to view Paul VI's body and then immediately began to work, not that there was much work to do. This time I couldn't leave as soon as the Pope died, so I will arrive not before the wake but at the very end of it, several days behind and with a feeling that I'm a latecomer and have a lot of catching up to do.

Rome, Thursday, April 7, 2005

The buzz here is that "stability and continuity" are essential in the present transitional time. The Curia and its allies always produce buzz in hopes of shaping the outcome of the conclave. However, this concern may be somewhat legitimate. As a priest who knows his way around remarked to me today, the last papacy crash-landed three years ago. He meant that no one has really been in charge for the past three years.

Moreover, no one wants another long papacy. Among the important tasks for the next Pope will be to devise methods for voluntary papal retirement and for coping with the problem of an incapacitated Pope.

I suspect that means the new Pope must be at least seventy-five years old — perhaps too old for the work and responsibility of the papacy (though Pope John was seventy-six).

The buzz concludes that the new Pope therefore cannot be from the third world, since all the third-world candidates are too young.

11:00 PM

There's constant babble of voices outside, almost all of them young Poles who swept into Rome today like another barbarian invasion — except they aren't barbarians, they are very nice kids. They have taken over the city. I exaggerate. Once you get away from the Vatican, it's not so bad, but I had a terrible time getting back here to the hotel after supper. The cabdriver dumped me on the east bank of the Tiber and wished me well, and it took about an hour of weaving in and out, coming back, going around in circles, climbing over fences, making dangerous jumps, to finally get back to the hotel. They're closing the city of Rome down tomorrow. No cars permitted in the streets because they expect several hundred thousand people at the funeral. They're going to close St. Peter's Square when a certain number get in, and everybody else will be lined up and down the streets or will have massive television screens at places like the Coliseum.

It will be interesting to see how much of the solemnity of the liturgy gets through. I don't even know whether it's possible to get over there and get a look at the funeral because some of the Polish kids are lined up already. They carry Polish flags, they sing

Polish freedom songs, and then they sing hymns in Latin. It's a very moving experience for them. They enjoy sharing this major moment in the life of their country and their Church with their companions. Many carry bedrolls; I don't know where they're going to sleep. There are outdoor toilets all around. I didn't encounter a single obnoxious young person. They were all extremely polite, a credit to their Polish mothers and fathers.

The rumors flying around about the conclave are disturbing. It would appear that both the Legionnaires of Christ and Opus Dei are out trying to manipulate electors and take charge of the commentary on what's happening. I don't know how successful they are. The *Corriere della Sera* reported today that Tettamanzi was down and Hummes up but that Ratzinger was coming up rapidly on the outside, and how the wise people thought that Ratzinger would win. Ratzinger, as I've mentioned before, is head of the Congregation for the Doctrine of the Faith, the Holy Office, a liberal at the council turned reactionary. He is willing to write off the whole of Europe as a bad bet and actually (as the Irish would say) he's by no means the worst of them. There could be much worse, and he might just take intellectual life more seriously than lots of these folks who are just interested in power and ideology.

Where all these stories come from I don't know. Not all the cardinals are in town yet and most of them are probably keeping their mouths shut. I suspect some Italian cardinals of leaking things to their friends in the media, trying to create an atmosphere. One of the things being said frequently, and this despite the *Corriere della Sera* article about Hummes's chances, is that this is not the time for a third-world Pope. I don't know what that means. I think it's absolute nonsense. Why not? If we could have a second-world Pope, a Pope who grew up in a Communist dictatorship, why can't we have a third-world Pope? Most of these stories are plants.

Once you get away from the enthusiasm and excitement of the kids, Rome is a pretty demoralizing place. Opus Dei and the Legionnaires of Christ, as I mentioned before, are out organizing things, campaigning, advertising, interpreting — all with the dedication, devotion, and enthusiasm that mark their groups (especially the Legionnaires). These are dangerous people. If Tettamanzi is the next Pope, they will definitely be in charge. I hope there are enough cardinal electors prepared to keep that from happening, but I am not convinced that this is the case. We're going to have to see how the stories come and go next week. Someone remarked tonight that this would be the largest funeral service in human history. Minimally, that shows that the Catholic Church still has a lot of vigor.

Well, that's about it for tonight, the end of a long, discouraging, but very interesting day. I'm exhausted. Twenty-seven years take a toll on one's energy. We'll just have to see what happens tomorrow.

FRIDAY, APRIL 8, 2005

It was, a local Jesuit told me, the largest wake and funeral in human history. And also, it seems to me, the most charming. It was therefore gloriously Catholic.

The Piazza of St. Peter's is filled. So is the Via Conciliazione from the Piazza down to the Tiber, as are all the surrounding streets in which the Mass is invisible but its sounds can be heard.

In other places such as the Circus Maximus, huge TV screens draw thousands more. The streets of Rome are quiet. The only planes in the air are Italian police and military helicopters. The city, however, is not solemn or sad. Catholic burial liturgy transforms sadness into something almost like celebration.

The charm comes from the hundreds of thousands of Polish young people who came to view the body of their hero Pope and waited for the funeral this morning, some of them carrying bedrolls and backpacks and the occasional guitar, and all of them extraordinarily well behaved. Many are dressed as if they were going to a pop concert and, like all young people away from home in large numbers, they are enjoying themselves. Some sweethearts hold hands. They are not solemn or somber, but they are always respectful of the time and place. They are never rowdy. Their only drinks are bottles of water.

When I was returning from supper last night, my taxi driver dumped me on the east side of the Tiber, not wanting to thread his way through the police barricades. Soon I found myself lost amid the crowds of Polish kids pouring out of the Piazza. Though we did not speak the same language, they were gracious and friendly to the poor confused Irish American priest and even helped me to climb a fence I shouldn't have tried to climb. Their mature behavior — almost miraculous in young people away from home — was a more powerful tribute to the Pope than was Cardinal Ratzinger's elegant homily this morning. They were not making a theological statement, they were offering a gift of loyalty and love.

The liturgy itself was superb Catholic theater in its baroque mode. The setting, the processions, the music, the vestments, the reverence, even the crimson cardinals' robes — products of the Catholic sacramental imagination, which sees such realities as signs of God's presence — created the mood of restrained hope Catholics adopt to cope with death. The presence of laymen and laywomen in the ceremonies, the exchange of peace, and the periodic bursts of applause reminded us that there had been, after all, a Second Vatican Council.

The power and beauty of the liturgy and the devotion of the young Poles were a fitting conclusion to the long and controversial papacy of John Paul II — and an appropriate reproof to the heavy-handed hype of some of the media who will never be able to understand the Catholic Church. We may be torn by controversy and dissent (which date back to Peter and James). We may have a hard time keeping up with history; we may sometimes be incredibly insensitive; we may even slip into corruption and sin (like the sexual abuse crisis); we may on occasion be monumentally clueless. We may be faced with problems that seem beyond solution. We may even mess up at the conclave next week. But we're not going away, we are not about to sink quietly into the trash can of history. We have resources and energy that many outside our community and not a few within the community don't understand.

We are a Church of community and Sacrament, both of which were on display in their full power and glory at the papal obsequies. We have always been that and we always will be. We've been around for a long time. We have endured for centuries external pressures and internal idiocies. We are not about to go away.

SATURDAY, APRIL 9, 2005

Almost as soon as the burial was accomplished yesterday, it started to rain, and it's been raining ever since. If one is to believe the weather report, it's going to rain every day next week. It's not supposed to rain in the Eternal City during April!

The papal funeral was an incredible performance and it represented, I think, the tensions between the Church of the Vatican Council and the Church of John Paul II. Joseph Ratzinger, the celebrant, is the principal heresy hunter of the Church and has made life miserable for theologians, and also probably put a damper on the intellectual life of the Church. On the other hand, it was an absolutely beautiful Mass, with the Sistine Choir, the elegant ceremonies, the cardinals all in their red, and the orderly lines of priests parading in and out of the basilica, all set in front of St. Peter's and within the embrace of the Bernini columns.

It was the baroque Latin Mass with some interesting additions — men and women bringing up the gifts, men and women reading the scriptural passages, the handshake of peace being exchanged enthusiastically by everyone in the huge crowd, Communion being distributed to everybody who wanted to receive it. And applause, applause often in the course of the liturgy, especially when the casket was lifted up to be brought inside the basilica and down to the crypt, where it will rest. Indeed, the congregation chanted, "John Paul Saint — Giovanni Paulo Santo." That may have come especially from the densely packed, wonderful Polish young people. But I think it was the whole crowd.

Some even shouted "Santo subito" — "a saint immediately," though *subito* does not necessarily indicate great urgency in Italian.

All these additions to the Mass represented the post–Vatican Council Church, though they may have been in conflict with what Joseph Ratzinger — who once supported all these things — would have liked. Maybe he didn't object. But the tension was there.

And there will be tension going into the conclave. The people who speak of Ratzinger as a serious possibility for the papacy are the ones who are bitterly opposed to the council and all its work. And if the electors permit themselves to be stampeded into voting for Ratzinger, it will be a kick in the teeth for those who believe in the council's reforms, who want to see them grow and flourish. It will seem to be an end of the Vatican Council. Of course, you can't end the effects of a Vatican Council or any other council, but it will be an enormous setback and a severe blow to many people in the Church — priests and laypeople alike.

The argument in favor of stability and continuity at this time is twofold: first of all, the Church is in crisis, and second, the demonstration for John Paul during the wake and the funeral proves that he was going in the right direction. I don't think either one of these assertions is true, but I'm not a cardinal elector. I suspect many of them will think along these lines. So on this rainy Saturday in Rome, I am very uneasy indeed.

I must say a word here about the Rome police, who did an extraordinary job of keeping everything quiet and orderly. All the Polish kids, of course, cooperated and were a great credit to their parents and to their religion and to their country, but still, with the hundreds of thousands of kids milling around, there was bound to be something of a carnival atmosphere. Even so, the Italian police set up an implicit working agreement with the kids, and the police were very polite and very firm. They blocked off streets so that when people began to emerge after the funeral they could easily find their way to wherever they were going. People were exiting from the funeral down our street for at least five or six hours after it was over. That's how long it took the crowd just to empty out. Even worse than a Bears football game at Soldier Field. And yet, it was all done patiently. They were tired, but they were smiling and talking and waving their Polish flags — all very impressive, as was the whole day.

The buzz around here is that it is not time yet for a South American Pope or a third-world Pope. That's a Curia line. When they say it's not time for something, they mean they don't want it. Of course there's no reason why if you have a Polish Pope, you can't have a Brazilian Pope. What they're afraid of is that the South Americans will come and take over their jobs and run the Church with a more left-wing orientation, which the Brazilian clergy and hierarchy seem to have despite the efforts of the Curia to get rid of the worst of the radicals.

There's more religious faith even in Europe than the Romans are willing to admit, including Cardinal Ratzinger. He still grieves for the lost Bavaria of his youth, which probably looks a lot better in nostalgic retrospect than it ever looked in reality.

I grieve for the lost St. Angela parish of my youth and even write stories often about it, yet I recognize nostalgia when I experience it and realize that there were many negative aspects of that world.

I am very upset at the attempts to put down a serious Brazilian candidate. There are 400 to 500 million Catholics in South America — 40 to 50 percent of the Church — and about two-fifths of them are in Brazil. That means Brazil has one-fifth of the Catholics in the world, and the Curia and Opus Dei and the Legionnaires of Christ and all these other people who are trying to shape the agenda will have you believe that it is not time for a Pope from those parts. Oh, it's time, all right, and it's past time for these people to be dealt into governing the Church at the top. Brazil has over one hundred universities and it's the eighth-largest industrial country in the world. It is an industrial country with an all-too powerful affluent class, a highly successful middle class, and its own internal third world. Brazil is not just string bikinis on Copacabana Beach or Carnival, though it is both of those, too. It's also the slums in the hills above Rio de Janeiro and in São Paulo and everywhere else. It's the movie *City of God*. Brazil is everything — it has five television networks and its own film studios. It's a great big exuberant, vibrant country. And if the clowns here in Rome don't understand the United States (and they don't), they understand Brazil even less.

In the week ahead there's going to be a lot of conspiracy to protect the status quo under the code phrase "continuity and stability." Many will try to forget that though John Paul II was a great man and in most respects a great Pope, he was unsuccessful in reasserting by fiat the Church's sexual ethic, and he failed to institute collegiality in the Church. He never seriously consulted with bishops on the ordination of women, he just announced that all the bishops in the world believed that women couldn't be priests. Well, how did he know? How many had he talked to? Contemporary Catholic theology is a very weak thing in part because people are afraid to get in trouble. The persecution of somebody like Jacques Dupuis, eventually cleared of all charges, was a signal: Don't do anything dangerous, particularly if you're a priest. If you're a layman, of course you can write anything — but we don't have all that many great lay theologians yet.

Well, this is my rant and rave on the morning after the Pope's funeral, as the rain comes down. I hope the Holy Spirit will manipulate events in such a way that the cardinal electors do the right thing once they go into conclave.

SUNDAY, APRIL 10, 2005

The weather continues to be very cloudy and gray, and the streets are wet from the rain. The *New York Times* reports this morning that the cardinals are saying we need a new Pope who can speak to the people the way John Paul did. The late Pope's holiness and personal goodness appealed enormously to the people, but I doubt that there's anybody in the whole Sacred College who really has the communication skills we're looking for. So, if that's what they're thinking about, they're going down a blind alley.

At this point, the cardinals are not supposed to talk anymore. They "unanimously" adopted a suggestion of the dean of the College of Cardinals, Joseph Ratzinger (*this was a mistake, for which I apologize later*), that they not give any more remarks to the media. They claimed that they should go through this next week in prayerful reflection as they prepare for the election. They still believe that they can do everything in secret and get away with it. It turns out that's not true. Jesus himself said that what is whispered in the closets will be proclaimed on the housetops. The most impressive result of secrecy in the contemporary Church has been the sex abuse crisis. Abuse was kept secret for a long, long time and then it became public and there was hell to pay. The Vatican Council's idea was transparency; the Church that emerged from it was supposed to be a transparent Church. But the Vatican Council is long gone now and its impact on people has been forgotten, so we're back to doing things in secret again — the old-fashioned way. Nobody seems to realize that this secrecy is counterproductive.

If you want a Pope who will influence the young people, you need him to be who he is in public. I'm afraid the cardinals are not going to see this. The sermons and the lectures that have been lined up are designed to produce a narrow and rigid Pope who will continue the status quo. The people who e-mail me from the States praying for another Pope John, for another Vatican Council, are going to be badly disappointed. The secrecy seems to me to be designed for a controlled conclave, one in which electors will not make the wise and proper choices for the good of the Church, but only those choices that the Roman Curia, or at least some of its members, think are best for them. Well, we shall see. I must not discount the possibility that the weather, the jet lag, and my general malaise are responsible for this pessimism.

Monday, April 11, 2005

The conclave next week will certainly be the most comfortable conclave in the history of this venerable institution. Cardinals might not even have to make their own beds.

The practice of locking them up was not originally intended to keep their debates and their votes secret. Rather, the idea was to keep them uncomfortable so that they would finish their work and produce for the Church a new Pope. After a couple of days, impatient folk on the outside would cut their food and drink to bread and water. In one case they took off the roof.

This tradition of discomfort persisted into the proximate past. Until the time of Leo XIII, the electors were forced to sleep in a dormitory. Leo (late nineteenth century) permitted curtains to separate the beds. In conclaves in the twentieth century, the electors were assigned offices and storerooms in the Vatican Palace in which each slept in a bed from a local monastery, sat on a single hard chair, and worked at a plain wooden desk with a single pencil and a tablet of paper. There were ten washrooms for almost a hundred men.

The late Cardinal Silvio Oddi, one of the more colorful of the men with red hats in the past century, described the sorry plight of elderly men, often with serious problems with walking and weak kidneys, who would hobble several times a night to the nearest john only to have to wait in line in embarrassed pain for their turn. To make matters worse, as Cardinal Oddi said, for the first time in many decades of their lives they had to make their own beds.

No wonder they felt great pressure to bring this purgatorial session to an end. No wonder the white smoke appeared quickly above the Sistine Chapel.

Pope John Paul II ended these harsh customs for men whose average age is in the middle seventies. The electors will be locked up in St. Martha's House, a "hotel" on the other side of St. Peter's from the Sistine Chapel that is used for various Vatican meetings. It is not exactly a rival to the Four Seasons chain. Yet each cardinal has a study and a bedroom with two chairs and, praise to heaven, his own bathroom. That's not even up to the standards of Motel 6, but it does provide privacy, basic comfort, and a shower of your very own.

The late Cardinal Bernardin remarked to me that the individual shower would transform the experience. Alas for him and for the rest of us, he will not be voting in this conclave.

I don't begrudge the electors comforts that are taken for granted in much of the modern world. I don't really think they will prolong the conclave. It is to the credit of the late Pope that he instituted this benign reform. And if they are a little slow in making a decision, well, someone could turn off the hot water.

However, I wonder if St. Martha's House may create new problems for the secrecy of the conclave. The cardinals will have to travel across Vatican City from St. Martha's to the Sistine Chapel — probably by bus. They will be in three different places instead of one, tripling the risk of bugs, which are much smaller and more powerful now than they were a quarter century ago. The Italian media will certainly try to find out what's going on, and other world media could try, too. It may no longer be technologically possible to hold a secret papal election.

Although I disapprove of the crookedness and cheating of those who would spy on the conclave, I'm not sure that secrecy is a good idea. Indeed, rigid secrecy only began in the early twentieth century. In earlier years the conclave was in St. John Lateran, and the electors used to walk down the street from their housing to the church and chat with people on the way.

What is there to hide? Why shouldn't the world know how the electors vote, just as in most other elections? Shouldn't the cardinals be responsible for their votes? Why not make a virtue out of necessity and adapt the policy of "open agreements, openly arrived at"? In the words of Pius XI, what does the Catholic Church have to fear from the truth?

The cardinals' "unanimous" decision to be secret even before they go into the conclave means they will not talk to the media until after the new Pope is elected. They ask the media folk to grant them privacy for prayer and reflection before they begin their heavy responsibility. That is, of course, their privilege — though the decision will not stop Italian cardinals from leaking information to their favorite journalists.

The electors will surely welcome temporary immunity from the media masses. With the exception of skilled public personalities like President Clinton, the Reverend Jesse Jackson, and Pope John Paul II, most people don't enjoy hovering journalists with their cameras and microphones. Yet the media play a critical role in a modern society. They make it impossible to hide. They impose transparency.

That's not the way they like it here at the Vatican. Secrecy is almost a religion. Cardinal Ratzinger runs his Congregation for the Doctrine of the Faith in absolute secrecy — though even that most solemn and sacred secrecy doesn't prevent leaks.

There are problems with secrecy as policy — it doesn't work, and attempts to preserve it often lead to disaster. The Lord Jesus said that what is whispered in the closets will be proclaimed from the housetops. I've never been able to figure out whether that was a description or a prescription. Probably it was both, a warning that you could never really keep something secret and it was better not to try.

Moreover, as the American cardinals ought to have learned from the pedophile mess, when your deepest and darkest secrets explode in your face, you are in serious trouble. If American Catholics hear that their leaders are doing something secret, they immediately become suspicious, and with good reason.

Transparency, in other words, is no longer optional for Catholic leaders or for anyone else. Public business must be done publicly, whether it be the reassignment of a priest with a dangerous record or discussion about who should be the next Pope. In both cases the public has a right to know what's going on.

Transparency does not come easily to anyone (especially if you're Irish, great folk that we are at hiding the self). It may be most difficult for Church leaders — of any denomination. Like academic deans, they are often inclined to hedge, equivocate, pull their punches, speak with forked tongues. How else do you keep everyone happy? They don't remember the injunction of the Founder that his followers should say "yes, yes or no, no." Not all the time, perhaps, but certainly when you're choosing the spiritual leader of a billion people.

The cardinal electors are very conscious of their obligation to God. I wish as an outsider that they would demonstrate that they are also obligated to those billion people around the world — through whom God's Spirit also speaks, given half a chance. I have heard none of them begin a statement (when they were still making public statements) by saying, "What my people back home are looking for is . . ." Yet the Church is those people and not just the officials who are permanent residents here in Rome.

I wonder if Ratzinger is running for Pope. Is he using his position as dean to showcase his own candidacy? His eulogy, his choice of speakers for the Masses for the late Pope during the next nine days, his "imposition" of secrecy — these certainly could be part of a personal campaign. Or is he just using his influence to facilitate a candidate who will agree with him?

TUESDAY, APRIL 12, 2005

The American TV networks spent huge sums of money and sent scores of people to Rome this past week. Characteristically, they spent little time or energy on research and hence provided weak and stereotypical journalism, limited to questions about married priests, women priests, gays, and sexual abuse. They missed completely the most critical issue for the Church in the twenty-first century — the Second Vatican Council and the changes it created.

Many, if not most, of the cardinal electors would tell you that the council was an incident, a bump in the road. The council fathers wrote some useful documents. There was misguided enthusiasm after the council, but Pope John Paul II sternly reimposed order on the Church. The council is interesting now mainly as a historical matter.

They could not be more wrong. The council was a revolutionary event that had a profound impact on Catholics who lived through it and indirectly on their children, who may have barely heard about it.

The council fathers voted for the changes in overwhelming numbers and thus embarked on a new spring for the Church — now flexible, joyful, and confidently open to the world. Some of the leaders, however, were frightened by the ferment, lost their nerve, and responded the only way they knew how — with repression. They issued new orders without any serious attempt to explain the reasons for them. They silenced some theologians. They appointed reactionary bishops, who were not always the brightest or most humane. They investigated seminaries. Their tone changed from optimism to grim warnings and solemn denunciations. The Church, for a few years a bright light on the mountaintop, once again became an embattled fortress.

The leaders confidently expected that the laity would do what they were told. They could not have been more wrong, nor their strategy more counterproductive. The laity and the lower clergy for the most part simply ignored them and went about creating new structures in which Catholics would affiliate with the Church on their own terms. Resignations from the priesthood and the collapse of priestly vocations began only after the desperate attempts to slow down the pace of change. The credibility of Church leadership eroded precisely from mistaken attempts to reassert the old leadership style. The problem was not so much the council as the subsequent restorationist attempts to undo it.

The restorationist style continues here in Rome, though it should be clear that it doesn't work. Despite the late Pope's efforts to reassert the Church's traditional sexual ethic, acceptance of it has declined everywhere, even among the young people in Poland.

In the preconclave atmosphere it is necessary to pretend that this is not true. Or, if there is a bit of truth in it, that the proper response of the new Pope should be yet tougher repression, more vigorous restoration. Almost no one is willing to admit even to themselves that the leadership strategy since 1970 has caused most of the problems in the Church — the decline in vocations and church attendance and the alienation of the young. They refuse to learn that you cannot repeal an ecumenical council and cancel out its effects.

WEDNESDAY, APRIL 13, 2005

The Italian papers began their own "campaign coverage" today. There are two groups, they tell us: the Ratzinger group and the Martini group, though the latter is not himself a candidate because of illness. In the Ratzinger group are Cardinals Ruini (Rome), Scola (Venice), and Schönborn (Vienna). In the Martini group are Danneels (Mechelen-Brussels) and Sodano (secretary of state). If the two groups divide the vote evenly, Tettamanzi (Milan) might emerge as the compromise candidate. Both groups can count on about thirty votes; though, depending on which paper you read, the Ratzinger group may be able to count on forty or fifty votes.

"Sex abuse, as terrible as it is," an American priest said here the other day, "ought not to be part of the media coverage of the conclave. It's an American issue and only a small part of the problems of the universal Church."

I figured my ears must be playing tricks again. Sexual abuse of one sort or another is, alas, a universal problem. It has existed always and everywhere. Sexual abuse of children by priests happens wherever there are priests and children. It has become a public problem in the United States (and other countries like Britain and Ireland where Common Law prevails) only because the American media and the American legal system have forced the Church to stop hiding it. For which I say thank God.

The crisis in the United States has revealed dangerous weaknesses in the structure and culture of the Catholic Church that exist everywhere and to which the next Pope must pay serious attention (not that I expect he will). How can the cardinal electors speak about finding a Pope who will appeal to young people if the Pope is unwilling to impose those reforms that will protect young people from abuse?

The current structures of Catholicism do not provide a system of responsibility and accountability for bishops — save for the ad hoc system existing now in the United States. Only the hapless Cardinal Law has been forced out of office for reassigning abusive priests (and is viewed here as a victim of the American media and activist laity). The existing clerical culture insists on the need to protect priests, at almost all costs. If Father Maciel, the founder of the Legionnaires of Christ, were an American priest he would have been removed from active duty given the strength of the abuse allegations against him. Here, as a personal friend of the late Pope's, he was immune from serious investigation. Recently Cardinal Ratzinger ordered a new investigation of the case, this time apparently a serious one, though he said it was a very delicate matter because Maciel was a friend of the Pope's.

A very stern Catholic dictum says *Ecclesia semper reformanda* — the Church must always be reformed. It is an absolutely essential rule for an organization that claims a divine mission but is made up of frail, limited, weak human beings — none more frail, limited, and weak than its leaders. Reform of secrecy, accountability, and a clerical culture that permits the abuse of women and children all over the world ought to be near the top of the list in the current agenda.

Cardinal Joseph Ratzinger has spoken of the "avalanche of clerical decadence" after the Second Vatican Council. He meant the resignation of priests to marry. Perhaps many of the men who left had not wanted to be priests in the first place. Perhaps the vocation was not theirs but their mothers'. Perhaps men who are not happy in the priesthood should be free to leave. There is far greater decadence in the sexual abuse of children by priests (which abuse is not caused by celibacy and exists in all denominations). I have not heard that Cardinal Ratzinger has fulminated in public against it. Yet it has done far more harm to the Church than all the heretical books that he has condemned.

Unfortunately, reform, however theoretically unarguable and practically essential, always encounters opposition from those who are powerful and have the most to lose. Reform of secrecy and accountability threatens to limit the power of both bishops and priests. The cardinal electors are bishops and priests. With the exception of some American cardinals who have had to cope with the abuse problem, I doubt that this kind of reform will be on the minds of many who go into conclave on Monday afternoon.

The pathetic demonstration outside of St. Peter's by members of the activist group SNAP against Cardinal Law earlier this week ought to be a warning to the electors. It was a small sign on the horizon that will eventually turn into a perfect storm unless drastic reform begins immediately. The SNAP people are very angry, as they have reason to be. The anger of American

Catholics on abuse is not just another crazy American fad. It could sweep the world like a forest fire before there is another conclave.

There was a time when one could make a lot of money out of a conclave. The ineffable Cesare Borgia (the model, it is said, for Niccolò Machiavelli's Prince, and played with wondrous malignancy by Orson Welles in the film *Prince of Foxes*) managed to buy nineteen of the twenty-one cardinals who voted in the election of his father, Pope Alexander VI. Pope Pius II tells us of the conspiracy to deny him the election by bribes handed out in the latrines, a deal he said smelled of the place of its origin. Buying and selling of votes in conclaves was routine until the end of the eighteenth century, especially by sovereign nations seeking to elect an ally — France, Austria, Spain, Portugal. Their money helped win the election of Clement XIV, who was expected to suppress the Jesuits and did so. Even in the early nineteenth century, the Catholic writer Chateaubriand was sent to Rome by the restored French monarchy with 100,000 livres to influence a papal election.

The reason for this investment in the outcome of conclaves was that the papacy was a genuine European power. The new Pope had at his disposal the coinage of corruption, money and jobs. He would appoint one of his nephews as the "Cardinal Nephew," who was among other things the dispenser of patronage. It was taken for granted that the Pope would make his relatives rich, some even as cardinals — including young men, like Sr. Borgia, who had no taste for celibacy.

With the collapse of the Papal States in 1870, reasons for such simony disappeared. If there were traces of this trade currently, it might make a good story, but there simply aren't any. The Vatican's endowment is less than that of a medium-size Catholic university, its annual income less than that of a major American archdiocese. St. Peter's and the Vatican Museums are loss leaders, barely breaking even on votive candles and admission prices. The Vatican is so poor that it had to take out a loan to pay for the second papal funeral in 1978. The only ones who might make money on the outcome of a conclave are gamblers who bet and win on a very long shot, like any American cardinal you might want to name.

Nor does a Pope have much in the way of patronage with which to reward those who supported him. Most priests from most countries are not eager to work in Rome. Some powerful archbishops may populate a country with bishops who are their underlings, as did Cardinal Law, but that was not because he had voted right in a conclave. Supporting a winner in the conclave can be dangerous. Two of the major supporters of Paul VI (Papa Montini) were Cardinals Suenens of Malines, Belgium, and Cardinal Lercaro of Bologna. The former was publicly humiliated (when he pleaded for more "collegiality" in the Church) and the latter eased out of office on fake charges of financial irregularity. The Pope later apologized to Lercaro but did not reinstate him.

John Paul II probably owed his election to the intervention of Cardinal Franz König of Vienna. Yet when it came time for König to retire, the Pope snubbed him and chose as his replacement a conservative theologian utterly unlike König. The new man turned out to be a child abuser and was forced out of the College of Cardinals. The next appointment was of a young aristocrat who belongs to the Dominican order and has made a mess out of Vienna.

In Chicago politics we have a saying: If you're not loyal to your friends, who (*sic*) will you be loyal to? In Chicago the mayor doesn't have much patronage to offer his allies, but he has a lot more than the Pope.

What, then, are the trade-offs, what is the grease that oils the halyards of the bark of Peter?

Some peripheral irregularities are troubling — such as the "tips" paid to lower- and middle-level curial bureaucrats. The late Cardinal John Cody greased his way to power by offering thousand-dollar bills with the injunction "Say a Mass for my mother" — a long way from the Borgias.

There is also the strong possibility, perhaps even the likelihood, that the new technology of electronic eavesdropping might provide the Italian media with vote tallies at the end of each conclave "scrutiny," not necessarily with the assistance of any of the electors. Should there be payoffs for this corruption, however, they won't be for the way a man voted.

Because there are so few rewards available, the conclave will presumably be about religion and religious leadership, at least as the electors define these subjects. Given the history of earlier conclaves, this somehow seems refreshing.

THURSDAY, APRIL 14, 2005

The Italian papers reported that the cardinals linked to Opus Dei — Herranz, Trujillo, Sepe, and Thorne (all curialists) — are now supporting Ratzinger. Big surprise. Corriere says that in addition to Trujillo and Stafford, Bertone (Genoa), Ruini, and Scola have allied themselves with the Ratzinger camp, while

Germans Kasper and Lehmann, as well as Murphy-O'Connor of England and Husar (Ukraine), are leaning toward Martini. They seem to agree that if Martini and Ratzinger and Tettamanzi deadlock, the way might be open for a South American.

Italian cardinals continue to violate the silence rule that the cardinals supposedly imposed on themselves. Cardinal Joseph Ratzinger, the dean of the Sacred College and perhaps the front-runner in the election next week, reportedly continues to beg the cardinals not to speak to reporters — seven times, according to one story in the Italian media. The journalist's source on the cardinal's plea for silence obviously broke the silence rule to inform about the plea.

According to another story, the Ratzinger faction has amassed at least fifty votes and would have several more if he promised certain Italian cardinals major curial jobs. Yet another story says that if he is not elected on Monday evening, Cardinal Ratzinger will withdraw as a candidate. Health dossiers are allegedly being circulated about Cardinal Scola's depression and the poor health of Cardinal Sodano and the diabetes of another cardinal — by their enemies, of course. Still another story reports that the American and German cardinals have vetoed the Ratzinger candidacy.

Should one believe any of these Vatican folktales? Is there that much wheeling and dealing going on? That much breaking of the silence rule? Or the rule against campaigning? Are there that many vicious personal assaults?

The story of a German-American veto of Cardinal Ratzinger seems especially suspicious. That Germans like Cardinals Lehmann and Kasper would be less than enthusiastic about their fellow German is not improbable. But that the American cardinals or even a group of them would exercise a "veto" is not likely — though in theory they might be able to.

One reports these stories as news and not necessarily as truth. It is the only news available in this time of alleged silence and illustrates the frenzy and the fantasy — and the occasional viciousness — typical of preconclave days. If there is no white smoke on Monday evening or Tuesday morning, we will know that the Ratzinger trial balloon, if there ever was one, has collapsed. I'm afraid, however, that he has it locked up.

None of the cardinal electors has asked for my opinion. Nonetheless, I'll offer it free of charge. They should choose as Pope a hopeful, holy man who smiles.

Most of us who are clergypersons of one sort or another seem to enjoy being grim and pessimistic. We delight in forceful denunciations, somber warnings, sweeping condemnations. We decry secularism, materialism, paganism, sexual hedonism, the "commodification" of life. We are most content with ourselves when we cause our people to feel inadequate, anxious, guilty, frightened. We are pleased when we leave them in fear and trembling, waiting for God's justice to strike them down like a thunderbolt from the sky.

Fair enough. Surely part of wisdom is challenge. The fear of the Lord is the beginning of wisdom. But only the beginning. Comfort is the other side of the coin of challenge, and perhaps the greater side. However, we are often reluctant to flip the coin. If we encourage and reassure our people, we feel somehow that we have failed them.

If we tell them, with Saint Teresa, that God is nothing but mercy and love, we think that maybe we have been too easy on them. If we say that they are God's beloved children whom he will never give up, we consider that we are encouraging sinfulness. If we argue that they are good people, flawed but still good, and God is hopelessly in love with them, we suspect that we're spoiling them. If we preach in season and out that there are grounds for hope, we are uneasy that they may lose their fear of the Lord.

Fear of the Lord is indeed the beginning of wisdom, but hope in God's love is the end of it.

Life is not easy. Humans must cope with disappointments, frustrations, blighted dreams, the tensions of physical intimacy and strong sexual desire, broken relationships, the stresses and strains of intimacy, sickness, sorrow, pain, impossible responsibilities, burdens beyond our strength, demanding children, parents, and employers, loss, suffering, emptiness, dread, despair, hatred, lust for revenge, humiliation, aging, ingratitude, seemingly irresistible temptation, and, of course, death.

No, not easy at all.

So when a religious leader comes along and praises us for our goodness, our patience, our dedicated love, our fidelity, and our generosity; when he tells us that there are grounds for hope, that our struggles are not in vain, that there is a rainbow somewhere, that life is stronger than death, and hope is stronger than despair, that human passion is a hint of God's passionate love; we say in effect to that leader, where have you been all my life? We may even say, isn't that what religion should be all about?

When a Pope in his glorious white robes becomes a beacon of hope and mercy and forgiveness, our spirits rise, our hearts beat faster, and we begin to smile, if only just a little smile.

Why are such leaders so rare? Is this not what the parables of Jesus suggest that a Pope or any preacher should do? Think of the parable of the indulgent father who forgave the prodigal son, though he knew that the young man was a manipulative faker; the parable of the farmer who paid a full day's wage to those who came around at the eleventh hour and did little but complain; the parable of the judge (Jesus, as the story is passed down to us) who absolved the woman taken in adultery even before she said she was sorry.

A Pope must of course condemn sin, must chastise evil, must deplore indifference. But I would suggest that when he has done these things, his job is only half done. He must flip the coin to the other side and show compassion for human weakness, understanding of human pain, and faith in the human ability to start over again, to renew relationships, to struggle on. The Pope must become the light of the world, the salt of the earth, the beacon of hope for struggling humankind. A Pope like that might not have the enormous personal charisma of his predecessor (a gift the Church is lucky to receive once in a millennium), but he won't need it. He will charm Europe back to religion; he will appeal to the young to sustain their enthusiasm. He will renew the energy of those in their middle years and bring laughter to the hearts of the elderly.

He will not be a hand-wringing Pope, but a hopeful, holy man who smiles.

Like I say, the electors are not running to me for advice.

FRIDAY, APRIL 15, 2005

The Italian media report that Ratzinger is blocked — though a couple of days ago they claimed he had more than fifty votes!

Tettamanzi has not picked up enough votes to become a front-runner. Hence there is a rumor about the Brazilian Agnelo (Salvador da Bahía), a man more liberal than Hummes. None of this guesswork should be taken seriously.

I want everyone to know that I have a Vatican press credential. I carry it next to my heart — well, actually in my shirt pocket, so that I can produce it at police roadblocks. Otherwise it is useless — it and two dollars will get me a ride on the subway!

I am one of the few journalists in town who were here at the conclaves in 1978 — which says something about either my durability or my folly. Many things have changed. The American cardinals now arrive with their media advisers in tow. The cardinals will live in nice quarters while in conclave. There are television tents all over the rooftops near the Vatican, none of them reassuring for someone with a minor inclination to acrophobia.

I must apologize to Cardinal Ratzinger for blaming the cardinals' self-imposed gag order on him. It was not his doing, and the cardinals are apparently very solemn and serious about their responsibility, except of course the Italians.

In one important respect, there's been a major regression over the last twenty-seven years. The Vatican Press Office is not as user-friendly as it used to be. A quarter century ago there were translations of important statements and sermons almost immediately. More critically, there were press briefings in many languages every day. Father Jim Roache of Chicago presided over the English-language briefings with such skill that even French journalists attended. He understood what journalists needed for their stories and did all he could to facilitate their work. More important, he was always candid. There are no such briefings this time around. Those who have only temporary credentials are not even permitted in the Sala Stampa (press hall) and are exiled to a satellite facility that is less lively than a wake.

Statements from Dr. Joaquín Navarro-Vals, the official Vatican spokesman, are rare and usually in writing. Although I congratulate him on the candor of his reporting on the Pope's deteriorating health — the first time in history the Vatican has reported truthfully on this issue — I must assert that the present silence is disturbing. The Vatican does not object to the brilliant infomercials on the Church that world TV presented last week. But it does object to the daily free flow of news. It does not seem to comprehend that in the world of the media, candor and openness — of the sort that Jim Roache represented twenty-seven years ago — are the only option.

Once the cameras turn away from spectacles, the world of the media becomes difficult and messy, but the opportunity for the Church to improve its image increases dramatically. The Vatican still does not get it. A charismatic Pope is only one part of the story; frequent and candid press briefings are the other part. If a media-savvy Pope should be elected, perhaps he could even have a press conference once a month. The opportunity to teach and preach to the world in such a context would be enormous. However, such opportunities cannot happen in a culture where addiction to secrecy is pervasive.

There is more secrecy this time around than there was a quarter century ago. The cardinals are silent and the Sala Stampa is empty. Perhaps this is the Opus Dei influence. Dr. Navarro-Vals is a member of Opus and there is nothing wrong with that. However, the secrecy that the organization believes necessary internally is certainly not appropriate for the Catholic

Church as it strives to improve its luminosity as the light of the world.

There is a long, long tradition around here of aversion to candor. It doesn't work anymore. It makes the Church look deceptive and tricky, and creates the impression that Catholicism is afraid of the truth. I can understand why an outsider would have that impression. Moreover, I am afraid that almost any of the candidates most likely to emerge under the white smoke next week will share in this addiction to secrecy. Nor will it likely occur to him that in countries like the United States, this addiction is an embarrassment to Catholics, making bestsellers of wild folktales like *The Da Vinci Code*.

It appears that the expected leaks from the Italian cardinals (and probably Opus Dei and the Legionnaires of Christ) to the Italian media have begun. There was an article in Corriere *yesterday saying that the General Congregation of the cardinals earlier that day was clearly splitting into two factions — one rallying around Cardinal Ratzinger and the other around Cardinal Martini. The Ratzinger group was claiming forty votes, and the Martini group thirty. Neither one of these is anywhere near the seventy-four needed for election, though* La Repubblica, *another Italian newspaper, claimed the Ratzinger group had fifty. They still have a long way to go, but it's a bit scary to think that a man who has written off Europe and rejects the effects of the Vatican Council (in which he was a major player) might be the next Pope, even if only for a few years. It would be a terrible sign to the world if a well-known heresy hunter ended up as Pope. I don't think it will happen, but today it does look a little bit more likely than it did yesterday.*

The news in the Italian papers shows that secrecy means one thing for Italians and another thing for Americans. Calvinists that we are, the American cardinals keep their mouths shut. The Machiavellian Italians take the promise of secrecy less seriously.

Martini was the last one to make an intervention at the General Congregation yesterday and he spoke for his allotted seven minutes. There was no one else to speak, so they gave him seven more minutes, and then finally, with no one speaking to reply to him, he got twenty-one minutes. I would suspect, knowing Carlo Maria Martini, that it was a dazzling performance.

The two factions are supposed to split up around Ratzinger on the one hand and Martini on the other. Ratzinger is, of course, a candidate for Pope himself, though he denies any desire to be Pope. Martini apparently is not a candidate. He is supporting, according to the paper, the candidate of his faction, which also includes Godfried Danneels and Angelo Sodano, the papal secretary of state (that is, the prime minister under John Paul II), a much more flexible and pragmatic man than Ratzinger. It's interesting that the curial cardinal would be considered more liberal than a German cardinal. It's also said that the other German cardinals, especially Kasper and Lehmann, are bitterly opposed to a Ratzinger papacy. I hope the Germans are out organizing their third-world clients.

Martini's remarks yesterday were apparently very passionate. He argued for more collegiality, among other things, and for better plans on how to deal with an incapacitated Pope. It is generally admitted around here that John Paul II's papacy crash-landed three years ago and that it hasn't been functioning as a meaningful papacy since. This, I think, has been pretty well covered up.

Anyway, the lines are drawn. I don't think either side is going to go into the first or second ballot with the majority of votes, the required two-thirds. Then they'll begin to look for a compromise. I'm not altogether sure that Martini can escape being a candidate. If his speech yesterday, "intervention" as they call it, was as powerful and dramatic as it sounds, then he's a candidate whether he likes it or not. The rivalry between these two men is fascinating. Ratzinger is a diocesan priest, Martini a Jesuit. Both are distinguished scholars, both are brilliant, both are multi-lingual, both are charmers. Ratzinger, though, has hardly done any pastoral work, and Martini was archbishop of what might be the largest functioning diocese in the world, in Milan — and levels of religious practice have been high all through his administration there. He's a wonderful television personality, continues to write books and articles, and fascinated the young people in Milan who used to come to the cathedral every Sunday night for a session with him. The negative on him is that he was certainly thought to be too liberal by the John Paul II regime. His resignation at seventy-five, they joke, was accepted by return fax, while many other cardinals who turned in their resignation at seventy-five were turned down. He may have a very early stage of Parkinson's disease, but even with a cane, he would be a powerful public figure. He's a Jesuit, and the only one in the whole bunch who could compare with John Paul II.

Neither Martini nor Ratzinger is in good health. Both are seventy-eight (though there's nothing wrong with being seventy-eight!), and neither one really seems to want to be Pope, though I think Ratzinger probably wants it more than Martini does. But I think if pushed into a corner, Martini would take it for the few years of life he has left in him. Neither would be Pope for very long. They would reestablish, as it were, the tradition of brief papacies — which isn't a bad idea, either.

Both men are a year older than I am, and my health, thanks be to God, is better than that of either. I haven't had a slight stroke or a heart attack and I don't have Parkinson's disease. Yet this reconnaissance to Rome and working and running every minute exhaust me. Why would anyone my age accept the papacy? Beats me!

Every conclave I've known has involved an effervescence of leaks to the Italian media. They rarely if ever predict who the Pope is going to be, so one has to view them with some suspicion. But it certainly adds a lot more liveliness to the proceedings and gives people something to talk about.

I went up to the NBC station today to do an interview for the *NBC Nightly News*. The interviewer was wonderful and we had a good time. NBC has four tents on the top of the Janiculum next to the North American College: MSNBC, NBC, Telemundo, and something else. Very professional operation.

Some years ago the government hollowed out much of the Janiculum to put in a huge parking garage and bus station. You walk into the bus station, get the elevator and ride up, and there you are. A beautiful day, beautiful view of the Vatican and St. Peter's and the square, and the mountains in the distance. If it's like this the day the white smoke appears, then it'll be very exciting indeed.

Incidentally, the smoke is now scheduled. They've timed it so that the media of the world will be ready. The white or black smoke will rise from the Sistine Chapel at 12:00 noon and 7:00 PM. So if reporters want to get over there, if the television people want to get their cameras set, they know the schedule.

This is a revolutionary idea. They never would have thought of that twenty-seven years ago, and it's a substantial improvement, though it may perhaps demystify the process somewhat.

What's nice about this innovation is that it shows some flexibility. It takes away a little of the drama, but the show is still pretty exciting. I could sit here in my room, if I really wanted to be cynical, look out the window, see the smoke come out, and then turn on the television and watch the rest of it. But I don't think I'll do that. I'll dash over to the Piazza. That's where I belong; that's where the real raw experience of the conclave is.

I reflect a little more on the notion of a Ratzinger papacy. It is quite unthinkable to me that this could happen, though given the makeup of the electors and the legacy that John Paul II left, I can't completely doubt it. It would be a terrible blow to many Catholics around the world, who would see it as a death blow to the Second Vatican Council and the destruction of all their hopes for change and improvement in the Church. It would be slamming a door shut, a kick in the teeth, a flat no to people's hopes. And if it happens, I'm going to have to say that reform goes on the back burner and stays there, however brief a papacy it may be.

I have to emphasize again that the conservative wing of the Italian Church has often managed to get rumors out before conclaves. At least at the two conclaves I experienced they did. In both cases, they floated rumors for very conservative candidates who weren't elected. So there's something inherently suspicious in their leaks — though in the absence of any more information, one can't help being fascinated.

The Italian newspapers are filled with contradictory reports this morning — largely, I think, unreliable. Martini and his allies are willing to settle for Tettamanzi in preference to Ratzinger. The Opus Dei people are out campaigning for Ratzinger. Yet other reports seem to say that some of the hot air has gone out of the Ratzinger balloon. Who knows? It all strikes me right now as being very problematic. It's the same way Giuseppi Siri won the last two conclaves, at least according to the prognostications of the Italian media. Some of this stuff may be made up out of whole cloth, but so much detail about campaigning (which is not supposed to happen) suggests that a lot of people are ignoring the silence that the cardinals are supposed to have imposed on themselves.

For the historical record I must say a word about eating in Rome. Between the passageway to Castel Sant'Angelo and the Via Crescenzio there are so many places to eat a good bowl of pasta and drink presentable red wine that someone who is prepared to lose five pounds on returning to America can have dinner every night at a different place at a reasonable price. For visiting clergy, the usual gathering spots are in and around the Borgo Pio, which is but one block above the passageway. However, one must exercise caution not to lose *la bella figura* — always important in Italy — by eating at a ristorante or a trattoria where everyone else eats. Definitely passé is the Ristorante da Roberto on the Borgo. There isn't anything wrong with the food. But Cardinal Wright no longer eats there (since he's long dead) and neither does Cardinal Ratzinger. Nonetheless, the place is filled with priests in various kinds of priestly garb and journalists who could do no better than a temporary credential from the Vatican Press Office, media advisers to the American cardinals, tourist priests, journalists who haven't found their way around Rome, clueless bishops (looking for a cardinal in disguise), and other people who are unaware of status matters. Jordan Bonfante invited me to supper there one night, unaware that the prestige scale had changed in twenty-seven years. I like it, too, because people-watching is more fun than status. The pizza with white cheese and mushrooms is to die for.

However, as I explained to Jordan, the top prestige ristorante in the area is Armando's, at the top end of the Via Plauto where it runs into the Via Vitalleschi. I only know this because John Allen, up-to-date on all things Roman, took me there one night with the *National Catholic Reporter* team. He insisted that I eat one of the antipasti, which I normally forsake out of an excess of virtue. It was alleged that Cardinal Ratzinger came in here often for supper, sometimes alone. There were two delightful happenings that night. The first was John's ordering the meal modo Italiano (which is why I never learned the name of the antipasto), with all the gestures and changes of voice that the scene demanded.

The second was the arrival of a tall, trim, handsome man in a bright crimson cassock, who looked like a character in a Fellini film. He saw John and strode across the room to greet him. The man turned out to be Cardinal Tarcisio Bertone of Genoa, one-time deputy to Cardinal Ratzinger and part-time soccer announcer for Genovese soccer matches.

The night was so delightful that I even indulged in some of the local gelato, which, as I tell everyone, is the second-best ice cream in the world — after the Russian, of course.

There's only one thing wrong with Armando's. The Scary Guys come there, too. They're the well-heeled, noisy American reactionaries who feel that they have power and money on their side and that if Cardinal Ratzinger is elected, all they need to do is turn over their hit lists and there will be a clean-out of the American Church. Some of them are commentators on the various networks these days and they snipe at the other commentators because if you can do something nasty, you miss an opportunity if you don't do it.

The Scary Guys don't wear black hats or even black shirts, though I think they might be packing. Like all reactionaries, they are filled with absolute moral satisfaction about their own righteousness and intellectual satisfaction about their own brainpower. If there is a reign of terror, the Scary Guys will hold the thumbscrews.

Anyway, I was there one night with Jordan Bonfante, sitting in the corner with my back to the door because it wasn't Chicago so sitting there wasn't dangerous. This crowd came in and made a lot of noise. I ignored it until I heard my name being taken in vain. They were in fact ridiculing me. I banished my demons, with some difficulty, and ignored them.

When Jordan and I were leaving, we encountered Jay Levine from CBS Chicago, who was sitting at a table by the door with his cameraman. He invited us to sit down and have another sip of wine. My sip, as the Irish would say, was little more than a splash in the glass!

I then turned around to check out those who despised me.

"Who are that bunch?" I asked Jay.

He told me that they were the Scary Guys.

Then my leprechaun, another variety of demon, took control. I walked to their table, greeted them with my shanty Irish smile, turned on my phony Irish charm, wished them good luck in their books, praised their work on TV (which fortunately I had missed), and departed as though we were all lifelong friends.

I left Armando's that night filled with a sense of my own virtue and the happy thought that they would never know (unless they read this book, which is most unlikely) that I had heard their conversation. I trust my angels were not too displeased with me.

I hope, incidentally, that if Cardinal Ratzinger is elected in a few days, he will maintain his apartment on the Piazza della Città Leonina, in the same building where I think my friend John Wright used to live. He could walk across the street to the Vatican or have someone drive him over. He could wear black and put on his business clothes only when he entered the papal office. He could continue to play his beloved grand piano at night. Occasionally he could join some friends at dinner in the Borgo. A Pope is entitled to a private life and recreation other than reading books.

If he doesn't do that (and he won't), then I hope he has the piano lugged up to the papal apartment. It would be good if the sounds of Mozart could be heard in the Vatican Palace.

Saturday, April 16, 2005

The Italian papers report again that Ratzinger will withdraw from the race if he does not win a majority of fifty-nine votes on the first ballot. They also say that Tettamanzi has about forty promised. Finally, they maintain that Cardinal George has opted for Martini. I trust I will be excused from believing any of that.

A few reflections based on conversations with people through the course of the day. One man I spoke to (Slovak in origin) said he had the impression that there was a Prague Spring stirring in the American Church, and he referred to an unsuccessful but promising Czech revolution back in the time of Brezhnev. He would perhaps more appropriately have talked about the Velvet Revolution of Václav Havel. But the suggestion was that there is this enormous energy and vitality in the American Church that would erupt if only some of the silliness and goofiness and authoritarianism and centralization went away. I can hardly disagree with that. Second, an English journalist who covered John Paul for some time said, somewhat sympathetically, that John Paul had only one possible style of governance given his background, and that was authoritarian centralization. This man didn't think John Paul really could cope with the problems of the Church, despite all his goodness and virtue and fine intentions. He said he hoped that whoever the new Pope was he would not be a sensational personality. He should be a nice man, and behave in public with some grace, but it wasn't necessary for him to be a charismatic leader or to attract big crowds. What was necessary for him was to present sympathetically and intelligently the Church's position and to be open to listening and learning. I think both propositions are true.

Am I concerned with the Ratzinger phenomenon? No. The Italian papers today seemed to suggest that enthusiasm for Ratzinger on his seventy-eighth birthday (today) has peaked and is now waning. Well, that may be true, but as always the source is dubious. The Englishman asked me what I, as an Anglo-Saxon, thought of the notion that promises of secrecy mean one thing to us and something quite different to the Italians. I replied that I was a Celt, not an Anglo-Saxon, but that I found it, to say the least, cynical and somehow wrong. American Calvinism believes that if you give your word, you keep it. We Celts are adept at hiding the truth, but we also believe that you keep your promises, one way or another.

Obviously, this doesn't seem to bother the Italians, who have no trouble when they have agreed to secrecy running to their own favorite correspondent and plotting things in the paper. I was curious this morning about why they were suddenly discussing a decline in the Ratzinger support. I don't know what that means. I hope it's true, but there's been so much nonsense in the absence of anything else that one has to listen to what the Italian papers say every day, even knowing that they have deceived us in at least the last two conclaves and maybe the last three.

Sunday, April 17, 2005

Today the Italian papers add Backis from Lithuania and Tauran (French, from the Secretariat of State) to the Martini supporters. They speculate that if there is a deadlock the list of "compromise candidates" will include such men as Schönborn and Castrillón Hoyos (Colombia) and their perennial favorite, Camillo Ruini. I suspect that they're right about the two factions and that the Ratzinger faction does not have the votes to win. When it comes to the "compromise candidates," I further suspect that Martini is serious about not being Pope and that when he withdraws it will be the ball game because his side cannot advance another presentable candidate.

The curtain goes up tomorrow night. It is one of the great reality dramas that human ingenuity has yet imagined — well, quasi reality, anyway. I have made it clear that I don't like the conclave as an election in which 115 elderly men select the religious leader of a billion people without any input from the billion. But as theater a conclave is hard to beat — crimson robes, secrecy, Michelangelo's *Last Judgment,* baroque setting, black smoke, black smoke, then white smoke, the great joy of *"Habemus papam!"*

The suspense, the uncertainty, the surprises, the effervescence at the end — no one could have scripted a better drama, yet it emerged almost as an accident of history, a charming and delightful anachronism, made all the more fascinating by the addition of the comfortable hotel in which the cardinals will live and the prospect of Vatican scramblers fighting electronic spies.

Today (Sunday) the cardinals may begin to slip into St. Martha's House, on the other side of St. Peter's from the Sistine Chapel. They must be there tomorrow. There will be a big Mass "For Electing a Pope" and then, at four o'clock in the afternoon, they will process in solemn crimson into the Sistine Chapel and begin to choose a Pope. There will be one "scrutiny" (which means two ballots), one burst of black smoke, and then they will return to St. Martha's House for a typically Italian late supper. The big game will have begun.

There are those who think that the smoke on Monday night will be white. They continue to predict that Cardinal Ratzinger will win on the first ballot. However, his supporters are less optimistic today than they were a few days ago (according to reports in the not always reliable Italian print media). His vote count, they admit, has been declining somewhat. More and more cardinals, especially the *stranieri* (foreigners), are allegedly saying the equivalent of "Not so fast, Louie."

I would not bet (today anyway) against a fairly long conclave and a surprise at the end. I hear more and more that Cardinal Ratzinger is a good and intelligent man. It is reported that he prevented an "infallible" decision on birth control on the argument that it was a subject to which infallibility did not extend. Yet one must worry about the impact on the world, Catholic and not, of the election of a seventy-eight-year-old man with the image of a grand inquisitor, an image he has done little to dispel.

The cardinals seem to be on the whole good men, quite overwhelmed by the importance of their task. They did not create and may not like the hothouse atmosphere of the work they begin tomorrow night. I cannot imagine that many of them were engaged in the frenzy of inappropriate and possibly illegal campaigning that the Italian media described this past week.

One used to be able to look up at the lights in the Vatican Palace at the end of the first day of the conclave as they blinked out and feel sad for the men inside. It all seemed too much. I don't know whether you can see the lights of St. Martha's House from outside, but it doesn't matter. It still seems too much.

I'm an outsider, yet I have a hard time sleeping these nights because of worry about the Church. I assume that many of the electors will toss and turn most of the night as the reality of what they're deciding sinks in. I don't wish anyone a sleepless night, but I do think they should be deeply worried about the Church, particularly about its credibility as a teacher, a credibility that has been eroding for the last thirty-five years despite the great personal admiration people felt for the late Pope. Credibility cannot be restored by force. In our times the only appeal the Church has is the rich beauty of its heritage. Contemporary humans cannot be ordered; they cannot be forced. They must be persuaded. They must, in fact, be charmed.

If the cardinal electors don't elect a credible leader (someone like my "hopeful, holy man who smiles"), a man who is firm and confident yet open and eager to listen and learn, the Church's credibility will continue to slip. The Church will survive, of course, as it always has, even in worse crises. But its light will not be as bright as it could be. No matter what the results, many Catholics will be deeply disappointed. Those who would like to see more openness, more flexibility, more consultation in the Church, will be angry if the winner is someone who favors an even tighter ecclesiastical discipline. Those who want the Church to be tougher with its enemies — Muslims, secularists, internal dissidents, decadent clergy, homosexuals, divorced and remarrieds, Protestants, Europeans, liberals, and just about everyone else — will be horrified if the new Pope shows the slightest sign of openness.

Personally, I'd be dismayed if Cardinal Joseph Ratzinger, the Church's official heresy hunter for a long time, is the next Pope. Nonetheless, if he is, he must be treated with the respect to which a Pope is entitled. Moreover, he must be given a chance to develop his own papal style. Everyone should remember that it is impossible to predict what a Pope will be like after he is elected. John XXIII was a nice little old fat Italian man who was supposed to preside over an uneventful transition. Nobody realized that he already had the scheme of an ecumenical council up his copious sleeve.

When Paul VI was chosen, everyone assumed that as one of the major figures of the Vatican Council, he would continue to be a man of the council. Yet in what many would consider a major tactical error, he spent much of his energy placating the most conservative of the Italian curialists who had insulted him in the years before his election.

John Paul II had been active in the work of the council, especially the document *Gaudium et Spes* (Joy and Hope), which presented an optimistic view of the possibilities of dialogue between the Church and the modern world. It was assumed that as Pope, this man of poetry, art, and philosophy would continue that optimism. However, he turned in the opposite direction and governed the Church with tight centralized control precisely to protect it from the modern world, which he repeatedly denounced.

My own hope is that if the new Pope is not Cardinal Martini, he will be someone from the third world who will open up new perspectives in this narrow, rigid place. Yet a "liberal" Pope can turn "conservative" when faced with the responsibilities of world leadership, and someone from the third world, isolated from his origins, might easily become more Roman than the Romans.

It is, one should excuse the expressions, a roll of the dice, a cut of the cards. Such a situation is inevitable when the electors do not know the candidates all that well.

There doesn't seem much doubt that this will be a very conservative conclave. The more moderate forces in the Sacred College are smaller than they were twenty-seven years ago. Those issues that seem to interest Americans — women, gays, decentralization of power, divorce, birth control — are likely to be ignored. Those who were expecting change would be well advised to forget about it.

Will Catholics leave the Church in the United States because the message is the same but the charisma of John Paul is absent? Women and gays, particularly, have reason to do so. But if the birth control encyclical didn't drive them out of the Church, then a new Pope who is unsympathetic to them will hardly do so.

MONDAY, APRIL 18, 2005

Il Giornale *lists the Ratzinger supporters this morning as Trujillo, Castrillón Hoyos, Medina Estévez, Ruini, Bertone, and Scola. It could well have added Stafford, Schönborn, Herranz, Sepe, and Thorne — and maybe Re if he received his promise that he would be secretary of state. That promise and the request for it might well be spurious. This is a formidable multicultural coalition. The only name added to the Martini coalition is Mahony of Los Angeles. Again I warn readers that the lists of supporters of either candidate must be treated not with a grain of salt but tons of it.*

Cardinal Ratzinger's "keynote address" in St. Peter's before the conclave began by attacking one of the primary assumptions of Vatican II — that the Church was strong enough and confident enough to be able to engage in dialogue with the modern world. The cardinal warned that the Church must struggle against Marxism, liberalism, libertinism, collectivism, relativism, radical individualism, and vague religious mysticism — the usual suspects — which bounced the bark of Peter on its dangerous voyage.

This outburst gives a hint of the way the minds of German theologians work. They observe a phenomenon. They define it.

Then they turn this definition into a reality with a force and existence of its own. Under such circumstances, there is no need to measure by empirical means the extent to which various forms of relativism exist and what effect they have on human life. In the absence of empirical evidence, "relativism" — pure and simple — is always the favorite culprit of conservatives.

Does Ratzinger refer to the relativism that says the taking of interest was once immoral but no longer is? The relativism that says that slavery was once moral but no longer is? The relativism that said all societies should have the same kind of Catholic liturgy and now says that "inculturation" of religion into a native society makes diversity of liturgical styles admirable? Or the relativism that says adultery is no longer sinful, or that it is no longer necessary to believe in the resurrection of Jesus?*

These distinctions seem to escape the German theological mind, enchanted as it is with the love of pure ideas.

John Allen suggested today that the Ratzinger speech was so over the top (my term) that it was clear that he was no longer running for Pope. I am inclined to think that he was so confident that he has the votes that he could lay out what many would see as a radical stand. If the white smoke shows up by Wednesday night, we'll know that my guess was correct.

I look out my window here and see the dome of St. Peter's and the Vatican Palace and the Sistine Chapel and the Raphael Stanza all clearly outlined, but what is especially striking is that

---

*In Appendix C at the end of this diary I cite a new book by Judge John Noonan, *A Church That Can and Cannot Change* (University of Notre Dame Press, 2005), about how the Church changed its mind on usury, slavery, religious freedom, and the indissolubility of marriage.

they've added the red drapes to the center balcony on the facade of St. Peter's the day before the cardinals go into the conclave. I suppose they're up there just in case Joseph Ratzinger is elected tomorrow night, in which case they'll need to have a *habemus papam* immediately. A somewhat discouraging thought, at least from my perspective.

The Italian papers this morning have backed off. They say it's going in as a deadlock, that the Ratzinger and the Martini factions both have about thirty votes; both of them are very far from the seventy-seven that are needed. We'll just have to wait and see what happens in that respect.

A couple of interesting comments heard today: one was that the American cardinals are going to have to work long and hard to put the spin on a Ratzinger election that will satisfy the American people. It's interesting that they would even be thinking in those terms. I suppose it's not that they're thinking what should we do when he's elected, but what should we do *if* he's elected. Another comment was that if you want to demystify the papacy, if you want to have a totally uncharismatic papacy, you elect a solemn German theologian who is devoid of charisma. One way to end the fixation on the personality of the Pope is to elect Cardinal Ratzinger. Such an outcome would take the papacy out of the news because he doesn't have the health to travel a lot. The things he might do or say would be heavily composed in the tones and the style of a professor in Germany.

So that's one of the good things that occur to me as I think about a Ratzinger papacy. That's about all I've picked up in the last twenty-four hours that seems pertinent to what's going on.

Probably it's going to be a longish conclave as the two main factions and the other factions' interests play the game of twisting and turning and putting together coalitions. I continue to be suspicious about the Italian newspapers and especially their sources. These sources have violated the pledge of silence and also the conclave norms against campaigning. They must be totally without conscience. That's why I think there will be attempts to communicate to the Italian media their ballot-by-ballot votes from inside the conclave.

This morning I went over to ABC to speak on *Good Morning America*. As we went up to the control room at the base of the platform, the technicians there said we couldn't use the platform because of the thunder and lightning, so we'd better find another way to do the interview. We went over to the European Union's set of platforms in the cold and in the rain at the base of the Piazza di San Pietro right next to the Sala Stampa. In the narrow quarters there, I managed to get on camera and say a few of the things that I thought needed to be said about secrecy in the conclave and about the dubious nature of the Ratzinger boom. As they say in Italian, *Fa brutto tempo*, meaning what awful weather, and yes, indeed, it is awful weather. The reaction from Chicago to my appearance on *Good Morning America* was that it was a badly done program but I did okay. Well, that was reassuring because in the cramped quarters, in the darkness of the rain and with the thunder behind, I couldn't even be sure if I was looking into the camera.

Jordan Bonfante told us at supper tonight that ten Vaticanologists from all over the world were asked to name their favorite and then a surprise favorite. Eight of the ten mentioned Ratzinger as likely; two of them, both women, suggested Cardinal Dias of India, who might be very good. Then they were asked to name their surprises, and Dias was heavy on that list, too. So the Ratzinger move continues, at least among the journalists and the Vaticanologists. I don't think it likely that Cardinal Joseph Ratzinger will be able to assemble the seventy-seven votes he needs to become Pope. Yet those who admire him insist that he is a good man whose public image does not do him justice, so I will repeat their case in the interest of fairness.

There seems to be general agreement that he is a good and approachable priest. There is no doubt that he possesses a brilliant mind. He wrote some of the best work on reform in the Church at the council and after. Like some of the other theologians of the council, he turned against it when he saw what he called an "avalanche of clerical decadence." I don't take seriously the argument that as Pope he would return to the openness of his younger years, but he is, make no mistake about it, a bright man who considers the life of the mind very important.

While his public presence is certainly adequate, he does not have the folk-hero image of the late Pope. There would be no cult of personality in a Ratzinger papacy. Moreover, for reasons of health he will not travel as much as John Paul II and will have more of a hands-on relationship with the Roman Curia, which he knows and understands very well — and which many felt John Paul often simply bypassed.

His spirituality is less romantic than that of the late Pope. He is not the kind of man who would ardently believe that Our Lady of Fatima jarred the hand of the Turkish assassin who tried to kill John Paul II. Similarly, because he is a professor and an academic, he would not accept personally the simplistic spirituality of some of the "new movements" in the Church, such as Opus Dei or the Legionnaires of Christ. These groups have strongly campaigned for him because they fear a Pope who would dislodge them from their current positions of influence. It is unlikely that as Pope, Cardinal Ratzinger would do that, but neither will he make them normative for the rest of the Church.

Many devout Catholics would recoil at his blunt assertion (which I quoted the other day) that it is wrong to say that the Holy Spirit elects the Pope because there have been Popes the Spirit would never have elected. He might also be less likely than some other Popes to identify his convictions with direct communication from God.

When it was proposed after the Pope's funeral that the cardinals be forbidden to talk to the media, Cardinal Ratzinger suggested that such a prohibition would violate freedom of speech and that if they wanted such a rule, they should, rather, unanimously adopt it — a technicality perhaps but not an unimportant one. It did not prevent Italian cardinals from talking to the media (perhaps through their staffs), but no one really thought they would keep the rule, which was enacted because the Italians objected to the presence of so many American cardinals on the international news channels.

He is also supposed to have persuaded John Paul that birth control was not an appropriate issue for an infallible declaration. Finally, the processing of the pedophile cases from the American bishops suggests that he and his staff are aware of the dimensions of the problem.

If one assembles these arguments into a projection of a Joseph Ratzinger papacy, one finds some reasons to believe that it would be quite different from the previous one, as Oxford don Owen Chadwick predicted in his "Law of Constitutional Elections"; the new man is always different from his predecessor. Maybe Papa Ratzinger would also be a different man as Pope than he was as the head of the Congregation for the Doctrine of the Faith.

Maybe.

This collection of arguments does not eliminate the fact that Joseph Ratzinger would come to the papacy with some very heavy baggage. Nonetheless, it does suggest that should he be elected (which, I repeat, I don't expect), he should be given a chance to prove who and what he is. When men become Pope, they tend to surprise both their friends and their enemies.

People write to tell me that we should leave it all to the Holy Spirit. I'm sorry, but that position smells of heresy. The Lord's Spirit works through secondary causes, through the actions and beliefs of human actors. I have not made it up, that's solid and traditional Catholic doctrine. The Spirit is the spirit of wonders and surprises, and it apparently delights in such outcomes of papal elections. However, the Spirit can work surprises only when there is enough openness and flexibility in the human agents. It is not fair to blame her (a pronoun Cardinal Ratzinger would deplore) for the mistakes the human electors have made repeatedly in the history of the Church. God may draw straight with crooked lines, but there are times when the human actors, in all good faith and goodwill, do not provide the raw material for God's artistry.

I don't mean that it does not matter whether Cardinal Ratzinger on the one hand or Cardinal Martini or Sodano or Hummes on the other is elected. It matters enormously. I mean rather that in the long run, often the very long run, the Holy Spirit will have her way. In the meantime, the Church will survive as it always has, no matter how badly.

As for the present group of electors, their eagerness to endorse the most reactionary elements of the Catholic heritage suggests that the Holy Spirit may have her work cut out for her in the short run.

Yet no matter what the outcome, no matter who is offended, one should not exclude the possibility of surprise lurking somewhere in the corners of the Sistine Chapel — along with the bugs that some cardinals may have smuggled in.

The Vatican itself does not trust all the cardinals. Yesterday, Dr. Navarro-Valls, the official press spokesman, escorted a group of his favored journalists through the Sistine Chapel. He asserted that it was impossible to send a cell phone message from the conclave. In fact, he challenged the reporters to try. Most of the calls were jammed by the devices installed in the chapel. But some got through. What does it say about the electors that the Vatican thinks some of them are willing to incur excommunication to make a cell phone call from inside the conclave? Whether the jamming devices will block electronic ears outside the chapel remains to be seen.

I would not be surprised if some of the Italian papers have ballot-by-ballot reports of the voting. This is a very cynical city.

LATER IN THE DAY

As I worry about what's going on inside the Sistine Chapel, I also begin to understand the pressures that weigh on the men in the chapel — at least those who are intelligent enough not to expect the Holy Spirit to whisper in their ears. They are expected to choose a leader for all the world's Catholics, when at best they understand only the religious problems of their own particular section of Catholic turf. Yet even in their own Catholic backyard, the electors are hampered by the poor mechanisms of upward communication in the Church. Many are clueless, through no fault of their own, about what's happening on their turf.

I cite as an example the problem of Catholic marriage, a problem below the radar screen, yet one that illustrates the difficulties of trying to restore the teaching credibility of the Church. In a study Mike Hout and I did a few years ago (national sample), we discovered that a third of Catholics under thirty-five who entered their first marriage to another Catholic for whom it was also a first marriage were not married in church. Eighty-five percent of them intend, however, to raise their children Catholic.

Their Catholic good faith seems to be established by the fact that they choose a Catholic spouse and want their children to be Catholic. Why, then, did they not have a church wedding before a priest and two witnesses, which has been necessary since the Council of Trent for the marriage to be a sacramental (and valid) Catholic marriage?

The data don't tell us the answer. I speculate, however, the reason is that some people encounter so many problems at the local rectory. We won't marry you unless you've lived in the parish for a year. We won't marry you unless you've been attending Mass for the last six months as proven by your use of collection envelopes. We won't marry you unless you attend a Cana Conference. We won't marry you if you've been living together unless you separate until the marriage. We won't marry you unless you can pass a psychological test that establishes your compatibility. We won't marry you unless you pay a stipend of one thousand dollars. Often the rules are enforced not by the priest, who is too busy to see the couple, but by a lay employee.

All these rules are a violation of canon law. Why do some priests try to enforce them? The reason might be that busy priests don't like to do marriages and especially don't like to put up with the demands of narcissistic brides and their mothers. The effect, though, is terribly damaging.

Some priests tell me that when a young couple shows up at their rectory, they have heard so many tales about these rules that they come in with a chip on their shoulder and are astonished at the warm reception they receive.

These problems do not loom large inside the Sistine Chapel these days. In fact, they don't loom at all. Even the American cardinals are not likely to be aware of them. Yet they loom very large indeed in the lives of Catholic young people thinking of marriage and of the priests who minister to them. They illustrate perfectly the disconnect between what Catholic leaders think is happening in the Church and what is actually happening. The leaders can (and some will) dismiss the young people who forsake a Catholic marriage as consumerists and materialists and secularists. Then, happy with their answer, they need pay no attention to the problem.

I would not argue that this issue should arise in the Sistine Chapel. I argue rather that, as the late Tip O'Neill said about politics, all religion is local. Like Willy Loman in *Death of a Salesman,* many of the cardinals don't know the territory in which their people live.

The man they elect should be a man who by instinct or personal experience does have some sense of local religion, of Catholicism at the grass roots as it impinges on the lives and loves of ordinary priests and people. I'm not sure that any of the electors would fit that job description. And I'm not sure that many of them sense that local religion is at all relevant to what they are doing. That's why I worry.

Some of the hate mail I receive from home tells me that I'm a sinner because I am not willing to trust in God's decision about the next Pope. Didn't Jesus promise Peter, the first Pope, that the gates of hell would not prevail against the Church of which Peter would be the rock?

Right!

At the time of a papal election one must ask, what did that promise mean? How can it stand up to the historical truth that there have been some very bad Popes?

The promise of Jesus is not that there will be great Popes all the time, not that Popes will necessarily be good men, not that they will be the best available choice for the office, not that they will speak for the Holy Spirit every time they say something, not that they will always reflect the wishes of God, but only that they will not destroy the Church. That promise has been kept, if only just barely on occasion.

The Theophylact family did not destroy the papacy or the Church, but they sure gave it a try. From 904 to 1048, Rome and the papacy were dominated by five generations of the Theophylact family. The gates of hell did not quite prevail against the Church, but it was, as Wellington remarked of Waterloo, a "near-run thing." One cannot reflect theologically on the papacy and not face this century and a half of history. It presents acute problems for those who argue that the Holy Spirit chooses each Pope deliberately and that the Pope is immediately and intimately connected to Jesus, for whom he speaks.

The Theophylacts were killers of Popes, bribers of Popes,

sons of Popes, mistresses of Popes, mothers of Popes. Five of them were Popes, none of them prizes, and three of them, John XI, John XII, and Benedict IX, made Alexander VI (Rodrigo Borgia) look like a saint. Installed in their teens or early twenties, they were given to gambling, drinking, adultery, rape, and murder. They plundered the papal treasury and pilgrims who came to Rome. The Lateran palace where they lived was reported to have become a brothel. They were alleged to have raped women pilgrims in St. Peter's. John XI is supposed to have died during an act of adultery. John XII was murdered, it is said, by an angry husband who caught him in the act of adultery. Benedict IX sold the papacy to a man who wanted to succeed him.

The most deadly members of the family were the matriarch, Theodora, and her daughter Mazoria, who ran both civil and ecclesiastical Rome for the first third of the tenth century. The former was the mistress of John X, whom she installed as Pope, only later to decree his death. The latter was the mistress of Pope Sergius III (at the age of fifteen) and the mother of John XI (of whom Pope Sergius was the father). In tandem these two women dominated papal appointments for thirty years, naming Popes, deposing them, and ordering their deaths. Mazoria was called the Senatrix of Rome from 1226 to 1232, while her son reigned as Pope.

Then another son, Alberic, overthrew and imprisoned her and treated his brother, the Pope, like a slave. Nonetheless, Alberic and his sons (one of whom became John XII, a man as bad as his uncle John XI) and grandsons ran Rome for another hundred years with the same iron hand as their maternal ancestors, until the emperor Conrad deposed Benedict IX, the great-great-grandson of Theodora and the great-grandson of Mazoria, and reform finally came to Rome. The power to name the Bishop of Rome was taken away from the priests, nobles, and people of Rome and given to the cardinals, a reform that was unquestionably necessary at the time.

Those were dark times in Europe. The Danes were raiding northern Europe, the Saracens had invaded southern Italy and sacked Rome. Rome was a lawless jungle. The German emperors tried repeatedly to impose reform on the city, but the Roman populace, mostly an unruly mob, would just as repeatedly revolt. The streets of Rome were dangerous both by day and by night. Power came from the tips of swords and spears. Anyone of prominence rose to power by the use of private armies and stayed in power through the strength of those same armies. The Theophylacts were no more murderous or corrupt or vicious or rapacious than any of the other nobles who lived in this jungle. They were only more successful. Given the times, the remarkable fact is that the papacy survived and that visitors like Otto I and England's King Canute had enormous reverence for the office of the Pope.*

---

*So, too, Lucrezia Borgia, who was not the promiscuous, poison-carrying stereotype of history but an intelligent, able, and devout woman (who spent at least a week every year in retreat at a convent). When she realized she was dying, she wrote in an extraordinary letter to Pope Leo X (Medici), a sinful man (who allegedly refused the last sacraments) and her political enemy, "Our most clement Creator has given so many gifts that I recognize the end of my life and feel that within a few hours I shall be out of it, having, however, received all the holy sacraments of the Church. And at this point, as a Christian, although a sinner, I come to beseech your Beatitude that through your benignity you might deign to give from the spiritual Treasury some suffrage with your holy benediction to my soul and thus devotedly I pray you; and to your grace I commend my lord Consort and my children, all servants of your Beatitude. Your humble servant, Lucrezia da Este."

One can certainly argue with some reason that the Holy Spirit preserved the papacy through these terrible times, no small achievement. But to see God doing much else during the reign of the Theophylacts is an insult to the deity.

Should we learn from the Theophylacts that the same thing could happen again? Hardly. But we might well learn just how human a Pope can be.

TUESDAY, APRIL 19, 2005

The conclave is in its first full day. They did take a vote last night and the black smoke came up. The general feeling seems to be that Ratzinger is going to win today on either the morning ballot or the afternoon ballot, and that will represent a decisive blow, not to my faith in the Church but to my faith in the things that have kind of organized my life since the Second Vatican Council. Pretty grim prognosis. Some of Ratzinger's supporters on the television stations — the American supporters — are making fun of the rest of us, indicating how confident they are of victory. Really nasty people. On this day when so much is likely to happen, my computer won't work. That is to say, I can't access AOL, the lines are always busy, so I can't send my dispatches off to the *Sun-Times*. I'll have to read them on the phone.

AFTERNOON

"Fuma è nera!" The crowd all want to see white smoke. They don't know what issues are lurking behind it. Three ballots have

gone by (two this morning), and Joseph Ratzinger has not been elected Pope. It's a gray day, not too cold, but not April in Rome as it should be. Huge crowd at St. Peter's. I turned the corner and was there a few minutes, looking for a *Herald Tribune*, which I didn't find, and then the black smoke came up, fairly thin black smoke but still black. The crowd began to drift away, an awful lot of people, more than in the last two conclaves. They'll really go crazy when the smoke is white. One of the Italian papers this morning said that there was a move to elect Cardinal Ratzinger last night by acclamation and that it failed. I don't know how they knew that, but I would say that if we last out the day, if he's not Pope John Paul III by seven-thirty tonight, then he won't be Pope. Mind you, as I have often said, these days he's not the worst of them and we might get one of the worst of them.

I've had terrible problems all day with my computer, so I'm a wreck. I woke up at seven, tried unsuccessfully to send my column off to Chicago, and rushed around all morning until about eleven o'clock trying to get functional. Finally, AOL decided to start responding.

I'm sitting on a cement bench at the head of the Conciliazione. It's 4:24 in the afternoon and crowds are pouring into the Piazza, because if the Pope is elected on what will be the fourth ballot, they'll put the white smoke up immediately. If he's not elected on the fourth ballot, then they'll have to vote again and maybe we'll have another day of conclave. My own personal anxiety increases each time I come over here. I haven't persuaded myself yet we're going to get through this day without Joseph Ratzinger as Pope. I will probably wait until about a quarter to five to see if the fourth ballot ends it, and then, if not, we'll come back at seven tonight to see again about smoke. The Piazza is jammed with people — tourists, priests, nuns, people in religious robes, people in black suits with Roman collars, older people, younger people, kids. It's a carnival, just as I said about the last papal election. Everybody wants to say they saw the white smoke. I hope it's not this afternoon. People from every nation under heaven are here: Americans, Austrians, Swiss, Poles, a group of Chinese people just passing by. And dogs barking, dogs not barking. It's ten to five. If there's going to be any white smoke, it's going to have to happen in the next ten minutes or we'll go on to the next ballot.

In front of St. Peter's, 6:15 PM

Ten minutes ago the smoke came up on CNN jet black, then it turned to gray, and the crowd down here were shouting "It is white," then about twenty minutes later, the bells of St. Peter's started to ring. So there's a Pope, almost certainly Joseph Ratzinger. We're at the colonnades now; it's pretty hard to get further in. Way up front, there are Polish flags waving, German flags, and the flags of the kingdom of Bavaria. The Germans are already celebrating. We moved our way up to the obelisk level, pretty close to St. Peter's. Huge crowds behind us. People came running madly up the Conciliazione as soon as they heard the bells. The obelisk is where Jordan Bonfante and I witnessed both the papal elections in 1978. It's a half hour after the gray smoke and fifteen minutes after the bells started to ring and the cardinal dean hasn't come out yet, senior cardinal deacon, to announce the name of the Pope — not that there's any doubt in anybody's mind about it. The sun is beginning to set behind St. Peter's, but there's also rain falling. I don't know why it's taking the medinia, the senior cardinal deacon, such a long time to get out to announce the name of the new Pope. It will be even longer before the Pope comes out to make his remarks, give his blessing.

The curtains are being pulled back; they close again. A cheer rises from the crowd. We're about to get an announcement . . .

Annuntiabo vobis gaudium magnum!
Habemus papam!
Reverendissime et Eminentissime Joseph Cardinalis Sanctae
Romanae Ecclesiae RATZINGER!

The crowd goes wild. There are lots of Germans here. The Bavarians are particularly happy.

Qui imposuit sibi nomen Benedicti!

He chooses the name of Benedict XVI. That he isn't John Paul III is a sign of some break. Benedict XV was a Pope who lived through the First World War and was generally admired as a very pastoral and sensible man. He didn't live very long, however. I think the new Pope is coming out. The German bands are going crazy. We hear them in the background. He's coming out and he's being received wildly by some people, though not by everybody by any means. There are women squealing as though he were Frank Sinatra.

190

His words are simple and modest. He imparts the blessing *urbi et orbi* (to the city and to the world) and retreats back inside St. Peter's.

The crowd is pushing madly to get out of the Piazza, the local Italians being especially brutal. People might get hurt. Italian cops are going crazy trying to maintain order, but they're not able to do it very well.

LATER

Why did the new Pope choose a name that only one Pope in the last hundred years used? Cardinal Giacomo della Chiesa became Pope in 1914 and died in 1922. He did his best to prevent and then end the Great War. Moreover, he put an end to the punitive campaign against "modernism" which Cardinal Merry del Val, the secretary of state under Saint Pius X, had unleashed on the church. Benedict was a healer who restored internal tolerance to the Church.

The Italian papers told us that you could tell what kind of Pope the new man would be by his name. If he chose "John Paul," he would be opting for a continuation of the late Pope's style of governance. If he chose "Pius," he would be returning to the middle decades of the last century, when the Church seemed frozen in place. If he chose "John," he would opt for the exciting years of the Second Vatican Council.

The new Pope rejected all those possibilities and selected a name that would distinguish his administration from his predecessors of the last hundred years *and* (perhaps) because he wanted to be known as a healer.

Heaven knows that there is need for healing in the Church. Perhaps a man whose conservative credentials as the head of the Congregation for the Doctrine of the Faith are unquestioned might be uniquely situated for the task — just as Richard Nixon was uniquely situated to open up to communist China.

Women — and not just in the United States — are very angry at the Church. It is no exaggeration to say that many of them, devout Catholics to the core, will tell you they hated John Paul because he hated women. If the new Pope wants to win them over, he will have a very hard sell on his hands. Similarly, gay and lesbian Catholics will find it difficult to forgive him for his comment that they are "objectively" disordered. He will have to put off his persona as stats professor and put on his persona as parish priest.

His own past rhetoric on many controversial subjects — liturgy, ecumenism, marriage — might stand in the way of healing, as would his attack on the modern world in his "keynote" address in St. Peter's before the conclave. There is certainly a gentle, pastoral dimension to his personality. If his goal is to heal, then he will have to rely on all the resources of that element of his selfhood.

Certainly he was most supportive of the American committee of the laity responsible for the sex abuse reports when they visited him. Unlike many others in the Vatican, he understood the problem and was horrified by it.

I may be reading too much into the choice of a name. There might be a reign of terror for those who still support the Vatican Council. I don't think so, but I could be wrong. Above all, he must come to understand, as his predecessor did not, that it is not enough merely to lay down the rules, because most Catholics in the world no longer concede the right of a Pope to make rules for them. If we did not want Catholics to think for themselves and make their own decisions, then we should never have permitted them to attend colleges and universities. Blind obedience is dead, not that it ever worked all that well.

To change the rhetoric from blind obedience to sensitive, charming, and listening persuasion will be no easy trick. Such a change, however, would bring the papacy more power rather than less.

Nevertheless, he *is* the Pope now and deserves the chance to put the imprint of his own views on the papacy. He won the conclave because — as the late Mayor Daley would have said — he had the votes.

Disagreements from the past should be suspended. Men become different once they see the world and its people from the perspective of the Throne of the Fisherman. Those who have disagreed with him in the past owe him the chance to develop what hopefully will be a serious ministry of healing.

His old protégé, rival, enemy, and perhaps friend, Hans Kung, weighed in with a commentary on the election of Pope Benedict that deserves to be quoted.

We must wait and see, for experience shows that the role of the Papacy in the Catholic Church today is so challenging that it can change anyone. Someone who enters the conclave a progressive cardinal can emerge as a conservative (such as Montini — Pope Paul VI), and someone who enters the conclave a conservative cardinal can, indeed, emerge as a progressive (Roncalli — Pope John XXIII).

We should note that the first signals of the present Papacy will be important:

1. The nominations to the most important offices in the Curia, above all the Cardinal Secretary of State and the Head of the Congregation of the Doctrine of the Faith.
2. The inaugural address, which will indicate the program.
3. The first encyclical, which will mark the way forward.
4. The first decisions about the organization of the Curia and further statements on questions of doctrine, morals and discipline.

The name Benedict XVI leaves open the possibility for a more moderate policy. Let us therefore give him a chance; as with any President of the United States, we should allow a new Pope one hundred days to learn. At every turn he faces tremendous tasks which have been piling up for a long time and which were not tackled by his predecessor:

- the active advancement of ecumenical relations between the Christian churches;
- the realization of the collegiality of the Pope with the bishops and the decentralization of church leadership, which is desired on all sides, in favor of a greater autonomy of the local churches;
- the guarantee of an equal footing for men and women in the church and the implementation of the full participation of women at all levels of the church.

WEDNESDAY, APRIL 20, 2005

Perhaps Pope Benedict XVI was elected because he had a good "organization," or what we might call in Chicago a "machine." More to the point, I believe, he was quite unintentionally the best asset for his own candidacy. I hasten to add that since one is forbidden to campaign under pain of grave canonical penalties, we cannot call his support a campaign — even if it looked like one and acted like one. Moreover, to be fair to the then Cardinal Ratzinger, he took no active part in it. He was perhaps something like the late governor Adlai Stevenson of Illinois — waiting to be nominated by acclamation before making a decision whether to accept. Indeed, the Italian media (not always to be trusted) reported that he would withdraw if there were not enough votes on the first ballot to promise victory. It would seem that he, quite properly in my judgment, wanted to avoid a bruising battle that would split the cardinals as they were in 1978.

Some months ago an informal group of the cardinal's supporters, Cardinals Stafford, Schönborn, and Scola, began to talk around the theme that he was the obvious man to maintain stability and continuity after John Paul died. Some of these thoughts were leaked quietly to the media, and they appeared, some almost using the very words "stability" and "continuity." Whether his supporters were sophisticated in media influence or not is irrelevant. The cardinal began to appear in most lists of the *papabili*, the Italian slang for front-runners for Pope.

When John Paul began to fail, members of some of the "new movements" began to spread the same ideas to anyone who would listen, providing interpretations for media personnel that contributed to the atmosphere that Cardinal Ratzinger was both the right candidate and a sure winner when the cardinal electors assembled in Rome.

I emphasize that there was nothing wrong with the behavior. Rather, it was intelligent politics — and as I have insisted, a conclave is an exercise in politics, in the art of government. Only after the Pope's funeral and the cardinals' imposition of silence on themselves did the murky business of counting votes begin. Each day of that week, the Italian media began to publish remarkably detailed lists of electors who had been lined up for the Bavarian cardinal. In the past such lists had proved wrong. This time they turned out to be accurate. As someone pointed out to me, "This time Marco [Marco Poleti, Italy's most famous Vaticanologist] finally got it right."

To Ratzinger's credit, his style of presiding over the General Congregations leading up to the conclave won him wide support among the electors. He was patient, gracious, and nondirective — authentically collegial, I am told. He knew the name of every cardinal and responded to them in their own languages. When they began to squabble about canon law, he is alleged to have responded, "We all know about canon law, but we must ask what is the best pastoral solution."

Two questions must be asked about the "non-campaign." Were cardinals violating the rules of silence they had imposed on themselves and the conclave rules that the late Pope had legislated and canvassing for votes? Were cardinals or their aides passing these tallies to local journalists?

Cardinal Ratzinger is reported to have begged them every day not to break the rules.

Regardless, the pretense of secrecy became porous. Behind the scenes precinct politics were taking place, which, if they did not shape Cardinal Ratzinger's plurality, certainly publicized it. His candidacy obtained momentum, and one hears today that after the first ballot (of four), there was almost no doubt about the outcome.

At the end of the first ballot the count was Ratzinger fifty votes, Martini thirty (or perhaps forty). Ratzinger's pledge to withdraw if he did not receive fifty votes was unnecessary. At supper, Cardinal Martini is supposed to have risen and announced, "I'm too old to be Pope."

If Martini had stayed in, might he have won? Or might Ratzinger have been stopped? God knows, and while he was certainly inside the conclave, he didn't have a vote. One must respect Cardinal Martini's choice.

That was the ball game. Some reports of the tally on the fourth ballot claim that he received ninety-one votes, others ninety-five. After the fourth ballot, Benedict XVI commented wryly that it would be a short pontificate.

In the pragmatics of electioneering, there can be no objection to the canvass of votes, the selection of a winner, and even the proclamation of that winner before the voting begins. The rules of secrecy and silence were, however, fractured. I conclude that the rules are a mockery and cannot be sustained in a communications society the likes of which exists in the contemporary world.

We do not know exactly who voted for whom on the first ballot and who contributed to the emerging Ratzinger two-thirds majority — though the names published in the press could provide excellent hints. Nor do we know who the campaign managers were who orchestrated the events of the final week. The first issue is not especially relevant. The second is important, and perhaps someone will find the answer. We also don't know whether the vote of Cardinal Re was obtained by promising him the job of secretary of state — as the Italian papers suggested.

Finally, two more questions: Was the "non-campaign" necessary, and was the Holy Spirit behind the outcome? Given the absence of an organization and a clear candidate among the progressives and Cardinal Ratzinger's "collegial" behavior during the General Congregations, the "non-campaign" may have been exhilarating but inessential. As to the Holy Spirit, as Cardinal Ratzinger himself has said, it is wrong to assert that the Spirit is responsible for the outcome of papal elections, because there have been Popes the Spirit could not have chosen.* Yet we can always pray to the Spirit to help and protect Benedict XVI.†

---

*Hate mail poured in to me, demanding to know the source for this statement, as though I had made it up as part of my campaign against the Spirit. Peter Steinfels, in his *New York Times* column of April 23, 2005, saved me the trouble by citing John Allen's book *Cardinal Ratzinger,* Continuum International Publishing Group, 2000.

†My analysis of April 20 is almost the same as that of Elena Curti in the April 20 issue of the *London Tablet,* though she faults the "liberals" for not running a better-organized campaign and for not having an effective backup candidate after Martini. However, once the majority of the Sacred College decided that the crucial issue was continuity and stability in the Church after Pope John Paul's twenty-seven-year administration, it might well have been impossible to find another candidate of the same stature and experience as Cardinal Ratzinger. As I said then, Martini, if he had stayed in, might have deadlocked the conclave. He made a decision not to.

Thursday, April 21, 2005

This morning I go up to the NBC tent on the Janiculum Hill to do the *Today* show with my old friend and fellow sociologist Cardinal Ted McCarrick. They have the two of us sitting next to each other but interview us separately, which is a shame because we could have had lots of fun. Ted is a typical smart, sharp, genial New York Irishman, which from me constitutes high praise. Katie Couric questions him first, as is appropriate. Then it's my turn. She is more aggressive than usual, which perhaps reflects the sentiments of many Catholic women in America. Her question hardly matters because I have an all-purpose answer. "Sure, Katie, I'd apply the old Irish compliment: He's not the worst of them. And if you ask me who the worst of them is, wouldn't I say that there's lots of them."

I go on to quote Hans Kung's theme that we must give him a chance and that the papacy often changes a man.

Alas, I couldn't see her face. I suspect she smiled.

Benedict gave a brilliant homily in the Sistine Chapel at the Mass that officially ended the conclave. It displayed the same grace and charm that marked his brief acceptance remarks yesterday. It's worth copying in full if only for the historical record.

Grace and peace in abundance to all of you! In my soul there are two contrasting sentiments in these hours. On the one hand, a sense of inadequacy and human turmoil for the responsibility entrusted to me yesterday as the Successor of the Apostle Peter in this See of Rome, with regard to the Universal Church. On the other hand I sense within me profound gratitude to God Who — as the liturgy makes us sing — does not abandon His flock, but leads it throughout time, under the guidance of those whom He has chosen as vicars of His Son, and made pastors.

Dear Ones, this intimate recognition for a gift of divine mercy prevails in my heart in spite of everything. I consider this a grace obtained for me by my venerated predecessor, John Paul II. It seems I can feel his strong hand squeezing mine; I seem to see his smiling eyes and listen to his words, addressed to me especially at this moment: "Do not be afraid!"

The death of the Holy Father John Paul II, and the days which followed, were for the Church and for the entire world an extraordinary time of grace. The great pain for his death and the void that it left in all of us were tempered by the action of the Risen Christ, which showed itself during long days in the choral wave of faith, love and spiritual solidarity, culminating in his solemn funeral.

We can say it: the funeral of John Paul II was a truly extraordinary experience in which was perceived in some way the power of God Who, through His Church, wishes to form a great family of all peoples, through the unifying force of Truth and Love. In the hour of death, conformed to his Master and Lord, John Paul II crowned his long and fruitful pontificate, confirming the Christian people in faith, gathering them around him and making the entire human family feel more united.

How can one not feel sustained by this witness?

How can one not feel the encouragement that comes from this event of grace?

Surprising every prevision I had, Divine Providence, through the will of the venerable Cardinal Fathers, called me to succeed this great Pope. I have been thinking in these hours about what happened in the region of Cesarea of Phillippi two thousand years ago: I seem to hear the words of Peter: "You are Christ, the Son of the living God," and the solemn affirmation of the Lord: "You are Peter and on this rock I will build my Church . . . I will give you the keys of the kingdom of heaven."

You are Christ! You are Peter! It seems I am reliving this very Gospel scene; I, the Successor of Peter, repeat with trepidation the anxious words of the fisherman from Galilee and I listen again with intimate emotion to the reassuring promise of the divine Master. If the weight of the responsibility that now lies on my poor shoulders is enormous, the divine power on which I can count is surely immeasurable: "You are Peter and on this rock I will build my Church." Electing me as the Bishop of Rome, the Lord wanted me as His Vicar, He wished me to be the "rock" upon which everyone may rest with confidence. I ask Him to make up for the poverty of my strength, that I may be a courageous and faithful pastor of His flock, always docile to the inspirations of His Spirit.

I undertake this special ministry, the "Petrine" ministry at the service of the Universal Church, with humble abandon to the hands of the Providence of God. And it is to Christ in the first place that I renew my total and trustworthy adhesion: "In Te, Domine, speravi; non confundar in aeternum!"

To you, Lord Cardinals, with a grateful soul for the trust shown me, I ask you to sustain me with prayer and with constant, active and wise collaboration. I also ask my brothers in the episcopacy to be close to me in prayer and counsel so that I may truly be the "Servus servorum Dei" (Servant of the servants of God). As Peter and the other Apostles were, through the will of the Lord, one apostolic college, in the same way the Successor of Peter and the Bishops, successors of the Apostles — and the Council forcefully repeated this — must be closely united among themselves. This collegial communion, even in the diversity of roles and functions of the Supreme Pontiff and the bishops, is at the service of the Church and the unity of faith, from which depends in a notable measure the effectiveness of the evangelizing action of the contemporary world. Thus, this path, upon which my venerated predecessors went forward, I too intend to follow, concerned solely with proclaiming to the world the living presence of Christ.

Before my eyes is, in particular, the witness of Pope John Paul II. He leaves us a Church that is more courageous, freer, younger. A Church that, according to his teaching and example, looks with serenity to the past and is not afraid of the future. With the Great Jubilee the Church was introduced into the new millennium carrying in her hands the Gospel, applied to the world through the authoritative re-reading of Vatican Council II. Pope John Paul II justly indicated the Council as a "compass" with which to orient ourselves in the vast ocean of the third millennium. Also in his spiritual testament he noted: "I am convinced that for a very long time the new generations will draw upon the riches that this council of the 20th century gave us."

I too, as I start in the service that is proper to the Successor of Peter, wish to affirm with force my decided will to pursue the commitment to enact Vatican Council II, in the wake of my predecessors and in faithful continuity with the millennia-old tradition of the Church. Precisely this year is the 40th anniversary of the conclusion of this conciliar assembly (December 8, 1965). With the passing of time, the conciliar documents have not lost their timeliness; their teachings have shown themselves to be especially pertinent to the new exigencies of the Church and the present globalized society.

In a very significant way, my pontificate starts as the Church is living the special year dedicated to the Eucharist. How can I not see in this providential coincidence an element that must mark the ministry to which I have been called? The Eucharist, the heart of Christian life and the source of the evangelizing mission of the Church, cannot but be the permanent center and the source of the petrine service entrusted to me.

The Eucharist makes the Risen Christ constantly present, Christ Who continues to give Himself to us, calling us to participate in the banquet of His Body and

His Blood. From this full communion with Him comes every other element of the life of the Church, in the first place the communion among the faithful, the commitment to proclaim and give witness to the Gospel, the ardor of charity towards all, especially towards the poor and the smallest.

In this year, therefore, the Solemnity of Corpus Christi must be celebrated in a particularly special way. The Eucharist will be at the center, in August, of World Youth Day in Cologne and, in October, of the ordinary Assembly of the Synod of Bishops which will take place on the theme "The Eucharist, Source and Summit of the Life and Mission of the Church." I ask everyone to intensify in coming months love and devotion to the Eucharistic Jesus and to express in a courageous and clear way the real presence of the Lord, above all through the solemnity and the correctness of the celebrations.

I ask this in a special way of priests, about whom I am thinking in this moment with great affection. The priestly ministry was born in the Cenacle, together with the Eucharist, as my venerated predecessor John Paul II underlined so many times. "The priestly life must have in a special way a 'Eucharistic form,'" he wrote in his last Letter for Holy Thursday. The devout daily celebration of Holy Mass, the center of the life and mission of every priest, contributes to this end.

Nourished and sustained by the Eucharist, Catholics cannot but feel stimulated to tend towards that full unity for which Christ hoped in the Cenacle. Peter's Successor knows that he must take on this supreme desire of the Divine Master in a particularly special way. To him, indeed, has been entrusted the duty of strengthening his brethren.

Thus, in full awareness and at the beginning of his ministry in the Church of Rome that Peter bathed with his blood, the current Successor assumes as his primary commitment that of working tirelessly towards the reconstitution of the full and visible unity of all Christ's followers. This is his ambition, this is his compelling duty. He is aware that to do so, expressions of good feelings are not enough. Concrete gestures are required to penetrate souls and move consciences, encouraging everyone to that interior conversion which is the basis for all progress on the road of ecumenism.

Theological dialogue is necessary. A profound examination of the historical reasons behind past choices is also indispensable. But even more urgent is that "purification of memory," which was so often evoked by John Paul II, and which alone can dispose souls to welcome the full truth of Christ. It is before Him, supreme Judge of all living things, that each of us must stand, in the awareness that one day we must explain to Him what we did and what we did not do for the great good that is the full and visible unity of all His disciples.

The current Successor of Peter feels himself to be personally implicated in this question and is disposed to do all in his power to promote the fundamental cause of ecumenism. In the wake of his predecessors, he is fully determined to cultivate any initiative that may seem appropriate to promote contact and agreement with representatives from the various Churches and ecciesial communities. Indeed, on this occasion too, he sends them his most cordial greetings in Christ, the one Lord of all.

In this moment, I go back in my memory to the unforgettable experience we all underwent with the death and the funeral of the lamented John Paul II. Around his mortal remains, lying on the bare earth, leaders of nations gathered, with people from all social classes and especially the young, in an unforgettable embrace of affection and admiration. The entire world looked to him with trust. To many it seemed as if that intense participation, amplified to the confines of the planet by the social communications media, was like a choral request for help addressed to the Pope by modern humanity which, wracked by fear and uncertainty, questions itself about the future.

The Church today must revive within herself an awareness of the task to present the world again with the voice of the One Who said: "I am the light of the world; he who follows me will not walk in darkness but will have the light of life." In undertaking his ministry, the new Pope knows that his task is to bring the light of Christ to shine before the men and women of today: not his own light but that of Christ.

With this awareness, I address myself to everyone, even to those who follow other religions or who are simply seeking an answer to the fundamental questions of life and have not yet found it. I address everyone with simplicity and affection, to assure them that the Church wants to continue to build an open and sincere dialogue with them, in a search for the true good of mankind and of society.

From God I invoke unity and peace for the human family and declare the willingness of all Catholics to cooperate for true social development, one that respects the dignity of all human beings.

I will make every effort and dedicate myself to pursuing the promising dialogue that my predecessors began with various civilizations, because it is mutual understanding that gives rise to conditions for a better future for everyone.

I am particularly thinking of young people. To them, the privileged interlocutors of John Paul II, I send an affectionate embrace in the hope, God willing, of meeting them at Cologne on the occasion of the next World Youth Day. With you, dear young people, I will continue to maintain a dialogue, listening to your expectations in an attempt to help you meet ever more profoundly the living, ever young, Christ.

"Mane nobiscum, Domine!" Stay with us, Lord! This invocation, which forms the dominant theme of John Paul II's Apostolic Letter for the Year of the Eucharist, is the prayer that comes spontaneously from my heart as I turn to begin the ministry to which Christ has called me. Like Peter, I too renew to Him my unconditional promise of faithfulness. He alone I intend to serve as I dedicate myself totally to the service of His Church.

In support of this promise, I invoke the maternal intercession of Mary Most Holy, in whose hands I place the present and the future of my person and of the Church. May the Holy Apostles Peter and Paul, and all the saints, also intercede.

With these sentiments I impart to you venerated brother cardinals, to those participating in this ritual, and to all those following us by television and radio, a special and affectionate blessing.

Everything is there that one hopes would be there, only somewhat limited by the rhetoric of ecclesiastical discourse — the council, ecumenism, collegiality, openness, dialogue with other religions and civilizations, willingness to dialogue, indeed, with practically anyone.

. As the late Pope would have spoken the same words, he would have attached a slightly different meaning to them than do most people (like me) who value the openness and the confidence of the council. "Collegiality" did not mean, for example, an end to authoritarian centralization or more serious consultation with the bishops of the world. It did not mean openness to dialogue with women (other than the women who had been preselected because they already agreed, so no dialogue was required) or with homosexuals or with priests who wanted optional celibacy or priests who have left the active ministry to marry and want to return as married priests. I doubt that these kinds of dialogues will occur in the new papacy. However, those who, like a certain conservative priest editor, are demanding that the Church in the United States be "cleaned out" (with himself, one presumes, as the principal broom sweeper) will probably be disappointed.

Conclaves are fun for outsiders and perhaps for some of the insiders, too. I enjoyed the nervous anxiety of waiting for the smoke, the confusion about the color of the smoke (they're still not able to get that right), the *gaudium magnum* speech of the senior cardinal deacon in which he tells the name of the new Pope, the appearance of the Pope on the balcony, the enthusiastic applause — mostly from Germans and especially Bavarians, much less from the locals.

I even enjoyed being caught in the crowd — Germans and Italians pushing their way out of the Piazza. I also enjoyed defending my tiny Celtic space with elbow movements refined on the outside parish basketball courts so long ago. It would be a shame to lose the conclave drama. Yet for the good of the Church it must be reformed.

In an earlier reflection I suggested that the conclave method of electing a Pope is corrupt. I didn't mean, as should have been obvious from the context, that either the process or the people who enter it were crooked but that it has lost the shape of an earlier era, that it represents a deterioration of the ancient customs of the Church as prescribed by Pope Leo the Great and Pope Gregory the Great. "He who presides over all should be chosen by all" (*Qui president super omnes, ab omnibus eligatur,* in the mother tongue).

In those days a bishop, including the Bishop of Rome, was nominated by the clergy, received by the people, and consecrated by the bishops of the province — raw and simple democracy.

This custom has survived in the Church in the election of

provincials, abbots, and higher superiors in religious orders. It works reasonably well, though often less than perfectly. The current method of electing a Pope is, for all its wondrous glamour and excitement, deficient precisely because there is no required "reception" by the laity and the lower clergy. This came to be (and it's a long story) because Rome had fallen under the domination of its own vicious noble citizenry and itinerant Roman emperors.

Hence the conclave as we know it is the result of a series of historical accidents. If *ecclesia semper reformanda* is true, then few of the needed reforms are more important than the reform of papal elections.

A couple of examples of the problems involved arose at the conclave earlier this week. First, in the brilliant TV shots from the Sistine Chapel, we saw that the electors were all elderly men in strikingly beautiful clothes. I have nothing against elderly men (or crimson garments), but I do not think they have a monopoly on the Holy Spirit, or intelligence, or insight. The words "by all" are hardly an adequate description of the process.

Moreover, because a younger and more vigorous Pope might live too long for the good of the papal office, there was the cruel election of a seventy-eight-year-old man with a history of heart problems and a bad eye caused by a minor stroke. Benedict XVI is a sacrifice to the Church's inability to assign term limits to the papal office. Moreover, it is evil to look forward to the early death of the Pope, as some Catholic liberals do. I wish to Pope Benedict, as we must to everyone, that he have a long and happy life.

How should the reform of the conclave proceed? The electoral base must expand, slowly perhaps, but inevitably. The sick and the elderly must not be sacrificial victims because a term limit for papal service has not been established. Secrecy this time was a charade and should be abandoned in favor of transparency.

The Church, I will be told, need not worry about the billion people excluded from the process. What do they know anyway? The Holy Spirit provides whatever outside input might be needed. Nor should the Church care about an intolerable burden for men who are nearing the end of their lives. If a Pope accepts the job and it kills him before due season, then that is his problem. We've always done it this way.

I remember painfully the experience in 1978 of sitting in a restaurant on Trastevere under the brilliant mosaics of Santa Maria and beneath a full moon with four friends and Bob Tucci, who was then director of Vatican Radio. My friends had seen John Paul I at the audience hall that morning and were taken with him. Andy Burd, a TV producer and director, was telling Bob that the Pope was a hot property. "Syndicate the Pope," he said enthusiastically. Bob admitted sadly that Vatican Radio had no TV capabilities. The next morning he phoned me to say that while we were talking about the Pope's being a hot property he was already dead. Bob is now a cardinal, too old to vote. In fact, he became too old a month after he was named cardinal. Too bad, he's a wise and good man.

Anyway, now they have a highly professional TV operation, the hardware at least (I am told) provided by the Knights of Columbus. Vatican TV — which the networks pick up sometimes, as in the procession to the Sistine Chapel — is very good, superbly shot and brilliantly directed. The closing of the doors of the chapel after all the *omnes* went *extra* was especially impressive.

The big screens they put up around the Piazza and elsewhere in the city were a first-rate communication technique. Why can't we always be that professional? The hardware is usually fine. It's the software and the content that's the problem.

Thursday, April 21, 2005

There's much talk around the Vatican and its satellites these days about the battle against secularism in Europe. It's reinforced by media stories about the decline of religion in Western Europe. Pope Benedict's principal battle, we hear, is against secularism. Or we hear that when he was still Cardinal Ratzinger, he had accepted the possibility that Western Europe was already lost and that perhaps the Church would be better off if it were smaller.

When they can put an "ism" at the end of a word, ecclesiastics are delighted. Now they have an abstraction that explains every problem. One need not attempt detailed research nor consider the possibility that failures in the Church's ministerial activity might have contributed to and even created the problem. We sociologists who have studied religion in Europe are powerless to counteract the appeal of an abstract shibboleth that has been turned into a reality.

In fact, there are three meanings that the word *secularization* has in contemporary usage. The first is that as societies have grown more complex, the Church has in part given up to civil society many activities in which it had to engage in earlier years — law enforcement, welfare, health care, and civil jurisdiction. The Church is no longer the only institution in society, but one of many and with more specified responsibilities than in the past.

Catholic Charities is still an important component of care for those who need help in the archdiocese, but it is not the only institution with such responsibilities, as would have been true in a medieval city.

The second and much more recent secularization is the loss of the power of the institutional Church to directly influence the decisions of governmental and civil organizations. In Ireland, for example, the Church had a virtual veto on government policy and decisions. Now it expresses its opinions quite humbly. In Chicago the last archbishop who had civil and political clout was George William Mundelein, who died in 1939. Closely related to this change is the decline in the ability of the Church to impose its teachings on the opinions and behavior of individual Catholics in political and social matters. Such independence of thought is the result of permitting Catholics to go to college and thus to think for themselves.

The third form of secularization is the decline of religious faith. The example that both cardinals and journalists love to talk about is France. In fact, one has to ask how Catholic France ever was and whether the countryside ever thoroughly converted to Catholicism — save in those areas where Vincent de Paul had his missions, which are still steadfastly Catholic. One must go further and ask how Catholic Europe ever was, even in the so-called age of faith. Research into the thirteenth and fourteenth centuries leaves considerable doubt that the Catholicism of Europe was either very deep or very devout.

Catholicism is still strong — if changed — in countries like Ireland, Spain, Italy, Portugal, and Switzerland, and in regions like Bavaria and Lombardia, to say nothing of Eastern European countries such as Slovakia and Poland. One would have added

Austria until recently, when the mistakes made by the last two archbishops on sexual abuse problems (which is an American problem, remember?) drove hundreds of thousands to formally disaffiliate.

Okay, religion in the Netherlands has collapsed, and in France it has never been very strong. It doesn't follow that there is no faith in Europe. Indeed, there was much more faith at the end of the second millennium than at the end of the first. Moreover, my own research shows that in eighteen countries (including France and the Netherlands), belief in life after death has increased with every successive birth cohort since 1945. This, gentle souls, is not secularism.

Pope Benedict and his allies in any attempt to preach the faith to Europe should realize that there is a lot of faith there. Moreover, the indifference and arrogance of Church leaders about religious problems and the needs of their people may well be a more serious obstacle than a platonic abstraction with an "ism" added to make it sound intelligent. Nor has the leadership's obsession with its own privileges and prerogatives helped. Before you preach, listen humbly. Before you give answers, listen humbly to the questions. Indeed, listen, and then listen, and then listen once again. Otherwise you will surely fail. And don't blame the people (or "secularism"), because it will be your own fault.

EN ROUTE TO CHICAGO, FRIDAY, APRIL 22, 2005

Three attractive and well-dressed teenage women were standing next to me in the Piazza. They were waiting for the first public appearance of Pope Benedict XVI. They had already exploded in joy at the announcement that we had a Pope. I thought this strange for Italians, most of whom were not particularly happy about their second straight loss of the papacy. When the new Pope finally appeared, they went wild.

"BE-NE-DET-TO! BE-NE-DET-TO! BE-NE-DET-TO!" they shouted in the rhythm of a European soccer chant. They screamed, they waved, they jumped up and down, they snapped away with their digital cameras and cell phones. Quite a greeting for an elderly German theology professor! These young persons reminded me of my own generation of young women — called bobby-soxers in those days — going wild over Frank Sinatra.

Does the white cassock and the crimson cloak immediately transform someone into a folk hero? Did the John Paul era mean that any Pope, indeed every Pope, would attract the attention due to a pop music star? I criticize neither the chanting young women nor, heaven forfend, the bobby-soxers. They both were celebrating a hero they admired — that's what young women do. (Remember Elvis?) This time it was a religious leader, so much the better.

However, that possibility raises the question of whether the Pope, almost by definition, enjoys an entirely new charisma — an immediate appeal to some young people. A second question follows on this day of Be-Ne-Det-To's installation as Pope: Given the inexperience and shallowness of the young, how much is this charisma worth?

I submit that it is a license for a Pope to teach and not an automatic guarantee of any other long-term religious impact. One heard often in Rome before the conclave that the new Pope should be able to communicate with young people like the late Pope did. Yet, in truth, the religious attitudes and behavior of young people in every country where there has been a World Youth Day have not changed — nor, for that matter, have the attitudes and behavior of adults in any of the countries he visited. As collective religious rituals these events were dramatic. They were a celebration of Catholic faith and Catholic heritage — and as such eminently effective. But they didn't change much in ordinary human life.

My three pretty, young Italian cheerleaders, unless they are different from typical Italian young women (as displayed in national surveys), will eventually sleep with their boyfriends before marriage and use birth control after marriage. They will see no contradiction between such behavior and enthusiasm for Benedict XVI. Does it follow that the new Pope should try to teach as well as celebrate religious faith when he attends the next World Youth Day in Cologne?

A majority of Germans who had an opinion were not pleased by his election. Kölners don't think much of Bavarians. In Cologne you're a Rhineland Catholic by birth and that is that. In Prussia, they say, people drink schnapps, in Bavaria they drink beer, but in the Rhineland, ah, we drink WINE! (and, truth to tell, a lot of beer too). Their initial inclination will be skepticism about this Bavarian Pope.

If he tells them that they should reform their sexual lives (not that there is any reason to think he plans to do so), they will simply laugh. Far better that he listen to them talk about their religious faith and urge them to be patient and forgiving in all their relationships and generous in helping others. Let sex wait for the next time or the time after. The reevangelization of Europe cannot be done all at once. This is what I mean when I say that youthful admiration for the Pope gives a license to teach — wisely, cautiously, and slowly, as any good teacher would.

My colleague Professor Charles Ragin of the University of Arizona has suggested to me in an e-mail today that there will likely be a Catholic revival among the young in Europe as a response to young Muslims — they have their faith, we should have a faith, too. With the leadership of a Pope who is skillful with the young, this might just be a *chairos*, an appropriate time, for a religious revival in Europe like the one in France in the second quarter of the nineteenth century in response to the French Revolution. But much more will have to go into such a relationship between Pope and young than the admiring chant of "BE-NE-DET-TO! BE-NE-DET-TO! BE-NE-DET-TO!"

CHICAGO, SUNDAY, APRIL 24, 2005

"Poor, dear man."

This favorite phrase of Irish womenfolk, both in the old country and America, flashed through my mind as I watched the Papal Investiture Mass at three AM on Sunday. He was graceful and charming, as he has been the last several days, but he also seemed weary and fragile and to some extent running on autopilot. Who wouldn't be in his situation?

So far since his election his moves have been flawless — the name Benedict with its appealing aura, the declaration of openness to all religions, his willingness to listen, his praise for the media folk, his invitation to rabbis (busy with the Passover) and Muslims to attend the investiture, the deep spirituality of his homily yesterday, his promise to Cardinal George about the sexual abuse problem. No one makes such moves under pressure if there is not internal grace beneath the external grace.

Benedict has given us a chance in the last couple of days to see who he is personally, just as in the preconclave homily he displayed his theological method and his fears of the ideologies that assault the Church and indeed humanity. As an American empiricist I am skeptical of such German Platonism. I agree, however, that there are a lot of enemies out there, many of whom the Church may have made unnecessarily. There are also many enemies inside the Church, too, more of them on the right than on the left.

The Pope's shift away from his early liberalism at the Vatican Council apparently is the result of student disorders at the University of Tübingen in 1968, a Marxist revolution as they saw it and as he saw it. Like most of the student uprisings around the world at the time, the revolution quickly disappeared because it was shallow and foolish. Most of the radicals of four decades ago have settled down to typical middle-class lives. In this country many of them have even become Republicans. Your Marxist revolution, as the Pope said to one of his colleagues years later, didn't work.

Naturally not. Revolutions don't happen in affluent societies that spoil their young adults with a period between adolescence and adulthood in which they can still pretend to be adolescents. I wish the future Pope had been able to see that.

He was also troubled by the behavior of priests and religious who reverted to an adolescence they had never experienced. He would later speak of an avalanche of clerical degeneracy — which is one way of describing it. I'd rather say that it was the shallow immaturity and intellectual weakness of those whose seminary or novitiate formation did not prepare them to cope with the changes in the Church that the council had occasioned. The real failure — both here and abroad — was that of their teachers and directors who wanted to keep them immature so as to better control their lives.

They went off to summer-study weeks or weekend workshops and became experts on theology, psychology, Scripture, sociology. They flitted from one fad to another. They flirted, paired off, and fell in love with one another — or what they thought was love, though in fact it was often merely a teenage crush. They were insufferable ideologues who knew the answers to everything, though in fact they were too superficial to understand even the buzz words they threw about or the authors (including Joseph Ratzinger!) they quoted.

I remember a quiet summer night on the shores of Lake Michigan when my cottage was invaded by three priests returning from several days of "sensitivity training" at the National Training Laboratories at Bethel, Maine. In their rootless enthusiasm one would have thought they had discovered the eighth sacrament. The late Father Jack Hotchkin, who was visiting me that night, argued with characteristic wit (God be good to him) for the value of insensitivity training that would provide one with the ability to say no to folly. In their eagerness to convert us, the late arrivals didn't even hear him.

Benedict will never read this reflection. Yet I would like to say to him this: Don't judge the late nineteen sixties by the crazies. Judge those years by those — the vast majority — who kept their heads on straight. The crazies are mostly gone now, one way or another, though some of them are still tormenting the lay folk as liturgists and religious education directors. Your early instincts were the correct ones. Don't be afraid to reexamine them.

Monday, April 25, 2005

Benedict XVI, I heard over and over upon returning from Rome, was responsible for John Kerry's losing the election last year. Fool that I was, I had not figured that out. I can't tell whether the story came from anti-Catholics who wanted to smear the new Pope (the same kinds of folks who made a big deal of his involuntary membership in the Hitler Youth Party) or fanatical Catholic conservatives who wanted to praise the new Pope for his good work.

The then Cardinal Ratzinger had written in response to a letter from the American hierarchy about Catholic candidates who supported abortion. Should they be denied the sacraments? And should Catholics who voted for such a candidate be denied the sacraments? The conclusion of the bishops' discussion of Cardinal Ratzinger's letter was that they would take no common stand but leave it to individual bishops to decide. The important point is that they did not decide to adopt the arguments of a few bishops that Catholics voting for Kerry should not receive the sacraments. The *New York Times* harrumphed that by not denouncing the stand of the few bishops when the rest of the hierarchy had approved it. One cannot, I suppose, expect a reporter for that paper to grasp that current canon law does not permit the total hierarchy from overriding the policy of even one bishop (as they may not override the decision of the bishop of Lincoln,

Nebraska, not to cooperate with the sexual abuse audit commissioned by the whole hierarchy).

The interesting part of Ratzinger's letter was a footnote in which he said that as long as they were not voting specifically to support abortion, Catholics could support such a candidate for proportionate reasons because then they would be engaging in "indirect material cooperation." The footnote in effect left Catholics free to vote for John Kerry if they believed they had a good reason to do so. This was a simple repetition of traditional Catholic moral theology — of which some bishops, many priests, and most Catholic conservatives were serenely unaware. Their response to efforts to explain "indirect material cooperation" was to say that there could be no proportionate reason.

What's proportionate or not must be determined by the individual conscience and cannot be decided by someone else. As far as I know, no one asked Cardinal Ratzinger whether the sacraments could be denied to a candidate who supports a preemptive war or the death penalty.

Moreover, an interesting award was made at the United Nations on September 19. Cardinal Angelo Sodano, papal secretary of state (prime minister) presented the Knight of the Grand Cross Pian Order to the outgoing president of the general assembly, one Julian Hunte — made him a papal knight. Mr. Hunte is the minister for external affairs of St. Lucia — one of the Lesser Antilles and a spin-off of the British Empire. Such an award was not in itself remarkable. The population of around 150,000 is 90 percent Catholic. It is a great honor for its people that one of their own should be in effect the president of the world.

However, there is a twist. Mr. Hunte cast the deciding vote in the parliament of his country in favor of decriminalizing abortion. He said, "A woman must be the one who will decide what she wants to do in any given situation. I respect the views of those who feel it is wrong. This is their right. I will give them that right, as I will give the woman the right to determine how she wishes to treat her life." This news was reported in the *Catholic Herald* of London and quoted by John Allen in his weekly column "The Word from Rome."

Should a Catholic university in this country want to give an award to Mr. Hunte, the local bishop would intervene to prevent it, as Cardinal Ratzinger ordered in his recent letter to the American bishops.

What, one might wonder, is going on? Are there separate rules for black politicians from the West Indies and for white politicians from Boston?

It should be no surprise to anyone who knows the Vatican that the various dicasteries tend to go their own way. Cardinal Sodano did not need to get Cardinal Ratzinger's permission for such an award and surely did not do so. As John Allen notes in his column, the secretariat of state normally chooses engagement with political leaders rather than confrontation. That the American Catholic Church has chosen the opposite is the result of a decision on the part of the American bishops, under internal pressure from their own members and from the pro-life movement. The implication in the award to Mr. Hunte is that, from the viewpoint of the most important office in the Vatican, that was not the only available choice.

While the bishops and priests involved in this campaign are relatively few, they have nonetheless created the impression around the country that the Church has become a wing of the Republican Party. This is not exactly an effort at persuasion.

How Catholics can vote for Mr. Bush, who doesn't really promise to end abortion, is not clear, save for the fact that Church leadership has always had different rules for Republicans.

Does one have to say that at the present moment the moral credibility of the Catholic Church is almost nonexistent because of the sexual abuse crisis and that the apparent effort to reelect Mr. Bush damages it even more?

In fact, Senator Kerry lost the election not because of "moral values," as the idiots at the *New York Times* proclaimed on the day after the election, but because of national security or the war on terrorism, the mantra that carried the President to another very close victory. Americans — especially American women — were more concerned about this issue than any other. Senator Kerry, having supported the war, found himself in a position in which he thought he had to say that he would fight the war on terror better than the incumbent could. It was not a very persuasive argument. Small wonder that the gender gap favoring the Democrats faded away. It is quite astonishing that Senator Kerry was only one state — Ohio — from winning, even with that handicap.

The leadership of the Evangelicals and of right-wing Catholics may claim that their "values issue" was decisive. They may use it to push their own agenda, which is the way the political game is played in this country. But they are not telling the truth (even if they believe they are).

It wasn't Catholics who reelected the President. It was white Protestants. Approximately two out of three white Protestants voted for him — without any help from Cardinal Ratzinger.

Catholics would have had to pile up an impossible plurality to counter that advantage.

Since I don't know whether this slander of the new Pope came from the right or the left, I will say merely that it took a very twisted and indeed evil mind to come up with the story that Benedict put Bush back in the White House — either a viciously bigoted anti-Catholic or a demented Catholic conservative who is eager to claim the Pope for his own cause. In either case it is a shameful story that, as far as I know, no one has bothered to refute.

I don't know whether Pope Benedict is any more or less "conservative" than his predecessor. I do know that he is against the death penalty and preemptive war and in favor of immigration and aid to the poor countries. Catholic conservatives should be careful who they are claiming for their own.

Concluding Reflections

JUNE 12, 2005

As should be obvious I was not enthusiastic in much of this diary about the possibility of Cardinal Ratzinger becoming Papa Ratzinger. Yet I find myself feeling sympathetic to and protective of Benedict XVI when so many people have already rushed to judgment.

I want to shout, "Give the poor man a chance!"

I don't add (usually even in my own mind), "Even if he is a German theologian!"

I have been amazed at the attacks on the new Pope since I've returned to America. He has been described as Hitler's Pope. He is blamed for John Kerry's defeat; his opposition to the use of condoms to fight AIDS has been described as a death sentence for two million people (as though the Africans pay any attention to what he says). Hostile editorials and letters appear in both the Catholic and the secular press.* The illusion has been created that one of his first acts was to fire Father Tom Reese, the editor of the Jesuit magazine *America*. Father Reese — intelligent, scholarly, witty, adroit. (Full disclosure: I consider him

---

*That ineffable representative of the Church Belligerent, William Donahue of the Catholic League, has instructed those who are not Catholic to "butt out" of expressing opinions of Pope Benedict.

a good friend.) Until his sudden dismissal shortly after the election of Benedict XVI, it seemed that he had satisfied the unease at the Vatican's Congregation for the Doctrine of the Faith about the controversial articles *America* published. Then suddenly, at the insistence of the congregation, the Jesuits removed him as editor. Does this mean that the new Pope will institute a reign of terror among American Catholics, a "housecleaning" that some fervent right-wing Catholics demand?

There can be no question that the departure from *America* of Father Reese creates a certain chill among some Catholic writers and publishers. There is a tendency to look over one's shoulder when one writes or speaks for fear of a secret note taker. This unease is increased when one hears that the removal of Father Reese was the work of a relatively small and secret group of American bishops, including at least one who is notorious for covering up pedophile cases. Among their complaints, one hears, is that Tom Reese used his platform as editor of *America* to comment on Catholic matters, which ought to be a prerogative of the hierarchy. Heaven protect, therefore, the cleric on television who is more articulate than a bishop. This secret clique of bishops, one suspects, settled a score with the Jesuits in general and Tom Reese in particular.

One might think, in passing, that if the Society of Jesus cannot protect one of their best from that kind of complaint, they might be wise to get out of the business of publishing a journal of opinion and commentary. Moreover, it might be asked if the Jesuits had given in too easily to the demands of the Holy Office. Yet it does seem strange that forty years after the end of the Vatican Council the arcane processes of anonymous accusations and secret trials continue. Is anyone safe? Do Church authorities realize what such star-chamber procedures do to its image among Catholics and others in this country? Do they care?

While the situation is troubling, I suspect that it is not as bad as it might seem at first blush. The Jesuit general decided to remove Reese in March when John Paul II was still Pope. (And good Jesuit that he is, he accepted it in obedience.) Despite the tendentious efforts of some American media outlets (most notably the *New York Times*) to depict his reassignment as a hint of the Benedictine papal style, this does not indicate that Pope Benedict will see the world the same way that Cardinal Ratzinger did — if indeed he personally signed the letter to the Jesuits.

As I said earlier, it can hardly be an accident that the choice of the name Benedict refers back to the last Pope of that name in the early years of the last century — who put an end to a particularly nasty system of anonymous denunciations.

Finally, Archbishop Levada of San Francisco, who will assume the presidency of the congregation in August, seems to understand what academic freedom is and to have had a good relationship with the Jesuit University of San Francisco. When asked whether he would be the new Pope's rottweiler (as Cardinal Ratzinger was called), he replied he would more likely be the "Pope's cocker spaniel." He knows the United States better than anyone else in the Curia and is not likely to be bullied by a secret cabal of bishops. Moreover, he finessed brilliantly a demand from the city of San Francisco that Church employees share benefits with their gay partners (by permitting the employees to designate beneficiaries whom they would choose).

Editors of magazines are especially vulnerable to the congregation. They are almost always clergy, and they are not protected by academic freedom as would be tenured faculty at Catholic colleges and universities, which are now often not owned by religious orders but by lay trustees. Lay faculties and lay authors, especially those at secular universities, are safe — and to condemn them would make their publishers' day. Catholic publishers who are not owned by religious orders might also light votive candles for a condemnation or two. The dismissal of Tom Reese, as appalling as it was, was not necessarily an omen of more to come.

Yet make no mistake about it, there are small covens of laity, clergy, and hierarchy in the United States who have a long list of others whom they want to houseclean.

There have been many efforts to explain Benedict to American Catholics. The *Commonweal* presents two articles on his theology that are beyond my understanding.

A priest friend has sent me a collection of quotes from Cardinal Ratzinger's work:

On Bringing the Church "Up to Date": "This attitude is very much like that of Pope John XXIII, who is supposed to have said of himself that he was the Pope of those who step on the gas as well as those who step on the brake. . . . This spiritual awakening, which the bishops accomplished in full view of the Church, or, rather, accomplished *as* the Church, was the great and irrevocable event of the council. It was more important in many respects than the texts [sixteen council documents] that it passed, for these texts could only voice a part of the new life that had been awakened in this encounter of the Church with its inner self."

The Pilgrim Nature of the Church and Its Need for Reform: "A Christ-oriented Church is thus oriented not merely toward past salvific events; it will always be a Church moving forward under the sign of hope. Its decisive future and its transformation are still ahead. It must therefore be always open to what comes and always ready to shed fixed formulations with which it was once at home so as to march on to the Lord, who is calling and waiting. . . . The Church, as the People of God on pilgrimage, is also always the Church under the sign of weakness and sin. It is a Church in continual need of God's forgiving kindness."

The Dignity of the Lay Vocation: "Theologians have to stop deriving the positive view of the layman [and laywoman] from nonecclesiastical and secular factors and must stop explaining the layman's position negatively. The question to ask is whether there are positive *ecclesiastical* categories in the Church besides those of the priest and the monk."

Liturgical Renewal: "We should first mention the return to Christian origins and the pruning of certain accretions often enough concealing the original Christian nucleus. . . . Mystery had to be restored to priority over devotion. . . . Ritual rigidity, which had almost obliterated the meaning of individual actions, had to be defrosted. . . . The liturgy had become a rigid, fixed, and firmly encrusted system. . . . There is and will be a stronger emphasis on the Word as an element of equal value with sacrament . . . : 'The treasures of the Bible are to be opened up more lavishly, so that richer fare may be provided for the faithful at the Table of God's Word' (*Constitution on the Sacred Liturgy*, nn. 51–52). . . . A special objective of liturgical reform, as was mentioned above, was a more active participation of the laity, the inclusion of the whole communion of God into holy fulfillment. . . . The Eucharist is there to build man up for the Body of Christ, and conversely the building up of the Church is accomplished through the Eucharist."

Papal Primacy and the Collegiality of the Bishops: "Peter remained one of the twelve. . . . He remained within the community and not outside of it. . . . Just as Peter belonged to the community of the twelve, so the Pope belongs to the college of bishops, regardless of the special role he fills, not outside but within the college. . . . Even the person indifferent to religion sees the papal primacy as an obstacle to the union of Christendom. . . . The unifying papal office remains in principle undiminished, although it is seen now more clearly in its proper context. The function of this office is not monarchic rule but rather coordination of the plurality which belongs to the Church's essence. . . . The question is whether this doctrine of episcopal collegiality has positive ecumenical value and whether it could be called pastoral, that is, promising for the Church's life. Closer investigation will show that both questions are identical in this case. . . . The college of bishops is not merely a creation of the Pope but rather a sacramental actuality — an autonomous reality stemming from the intrinsic nature of the Church."

The "Problem of Centralism in the Church" and the Need to Respect Pluralism: "The Church was no longer seen in terms of political models but in terms of biblical images. . . . A fabric of worshipping congregations shows [that] unity consists in the essential unity of divine worship and the faith expressed in that worship. . . .

This plurality constitutes the inner structure of the one Church. Within the unity of the Church, a relative degree of autonomy belongs to the individual churches, which normally consist of a larger group of diocesan churches. This independence will express itself in liturgical as well as administrative matters. . . . It was now as never before unmistakably clear that the Church had become an international Church, drawing on the treasures of all nations, and showing the meaning of plurality within the unity of the Church. . . . I believe that this rediscovery of the local [diocesan] Church is one of the most significant and pertinent statements of the doctrine of collegiality, for it again becomes clear that the *one* Church comprises the plurality of the churches, that unity and multiplicity are not contradictions in the Church."

Ecumenism and Interfaith Dialogue: "Ecumenism also was to be found in the view of ecclesiastical offices as ministry, of laymen as within the framework of the unity of the holy People of God, and of holiness as a gift God continually gives to a Church in constant need of forgiveness. . . . The new text [of the "Dogmatic Constitution on the Church"] now says unmistakably and clearly, although in passing, that these [Protestant] Christians exist not merely as *individuals* but in Christian communities which are given positive Christian status and ecclesial status. . . . Now that we are used to this attitude, we take it in stride."

The "Option for the Poor": "It was especially the Latin [American] countries that developed the idea that the Church is the 'Church of the Poor.' . . . In 1962 [the Latin American churches] had become independent collaborators in the work of renewal, from which they expected an answer to urgent needs in a situation full of danger and full of hope."

On "Factionalism" Within the Church: "Any success in this regard [on ongoing church renewal] may be frustrated, not only by the opposition of those who are called, perhaps a little condescendingly, 'conservatives.' (Incidentally, their sincerity and the need for their services should not be called into question. I hope it has been evident, at least to some extent, in our discussion that their objections were by no means pointless, but rather in many respects very worthy of consideration.) . . . What has been granted us in this [Second Vatican] Council involves also a mission and a challenge — one that will require great patience, the patience which comes from faith."

The Primacy of Conscience: "The criterion of [Pope Paul VI's 1968 encyclical] *Humanae Vitae,* clear as it is, is not inflexible but open for differentiated judgments of ethically differentiated situations."

Admittedly all of these quotes, save the last one, date from the time when Cardinal Ratzinger had not undergone his theological reorientation as a result of the 1968 student unrest. It is not likely that he will return to most of these positions of his youth. The last one, however, was spoken when he was archbishop of Munich, long after his reorientation.

Robert McClory, in an article in the *Chicago Tribune,* compares Ratzinger's statements from 1972 and 1994 on Communion for divorced and remarried Catholics:

(1972) It seems that the grant of full Communions after a time of probation is nothing less than just and is fully in harmony with our ecclesiastical traditions.

(1994) Remarried Catholics are in a situation that objectively contravenes God's law; consequently they cannot receive Holy Communion as long as this situation persists.

McClory also cites a comment in a 1969 book — published a year after the birth control encyclical — about what would happen if an officially proclaimed doctrine, even one proclaimed infallibly, were to be rejected by a significant group of Catholics. Ratzinger's reply:

Where there is neither consensus on the part of the universal church nor clear testimony in the sources, no binding position is possible. If such a decision were formally made, it would meet the necessary conditions, and the question of the decision's legitimacy would have to be examined.

A person is certainly allowed to change his mind. Perhaps it would be useful if a man who has apparently so dramatically changed his mind could explain why he did so.

One gathers that the reason for the change might have been his fear that authority in the Church was losing its power and needed to be reaffirmed. Preserving the authority of Church leaders is absolutely essential. But in the world in which we live, effective authority is the ability to obtain consent.

That means — at the risk of repeating once again a major theme of this book — listening carefully to those whose consent you want to obtain.

John Allen, in his June 3, 2005, column° The Word from Rome, describes the new Pope's "ambition to challenge four centuries of intellectual development in the West toward subjectivity and relativism." I found this summary more lucid than the *Commonweal* articles. However, the Pope's agenda sounds very much like that of a German theologian — abstract, theoretical, unrelated to the reality of Christian life (though not necessarily wrong). I would much rather know what kind of bishop he will send to the United States — more intelligent men such as Archbishop Levada or more of the recent amadons that have appeared here. Who will he send to Washington, D.C., for example, to replace the marvelous Ted McCarrick? Will it really be Archbishop Chaput of Denver, the leader in the deny-Communion campaign during the last election?

In short, I continue to agree with Hans Kung that Pope Benedict should be given more time before any definitive conclusions are reached about his work. It seems clear, however, that many Americans, Catholic and not, are not prepared to grant him that time.

Those pious Catholics who insist that God has already chosen the winner before the conclave (as one cardinal elector said upon arrival in Rome) or that the Holy Spirit inspires the electors how to vote are guilty of both ignorance of history and gross

°Out of fairness to John, I will not read the revised edition of his biography of Cardinal Ratzinger, which brings the book up to date, until my book is locked into production. Whatever dialogue I have with him about the book will be private.

idolatry. God's spirit works through human actors and guarantees nothing, save the survival of the Church. In the words of the old Irish monsignor, "There must be something special about the Church, otherwise we lads would have kicked the bottom out long ago."

The secrecy of the conclave is a farce and will be a farce as long as there are Italian cardinals involved. It was simplicity itself to pick up the story of what went on inside. Indeed, if one had kept the editions of *Corriere* handy, one could have listed the two factions with ease. The pledge not to talk to the media during the General Congregations was also a farce. Whether there would have been attempts to penetrate the jamming system in the Sistine Chapel if the conclave had lasted more than four ballots is an interesting question. Secrecy doesn't work. It provides a little bit of drama in the white smoke symbol, but it is not worth the price.

Incidentally, they weren't able to make the white smoke work again this time. The Cardinal Fire Starter bungled the task, sent gray smoke up the chimney, and filled half the Sistine Chapel with the white smoke. Cardinal Schönborn commented that he hoped the art historians never found out.

Some way must be found to expand the voting base, so that the electors of the Pope are not an elderly oligarchy and that the ancient norm of *ab omnibus eligatur* can be honored. Even if the electors produced by the current rules were the most brilliant men in Christendom — and no one claims that they are — it is not seemly, not appropriate, and eventually not even Catholic for the *omnes* to be ignored. Paul VI's scheme to invite the presidents of the national conferences of bishops to participate — to perhaps become ad hoc cardinals — might be a good way to start. It is also a very serious problem that slightly more than half the human race, all the women of the world, are excluded.

I am under no illusion that anyone in power and authority will listen to my suggestions. However, I must make them or I will feel my time in Rome was wasted. The present making of the Pope does not work. Saints Leo and Gregory would also have said that the system was unjust.

I was probably unjust in my early judgments about Cardinal Ratzinger. I could plead that I didn't know him. But somehow I did know him. A man depicted in my novel *An Occasion of Sin*, the lunch mate of protagonist Father Laurence O'Toole McAuliffe, was the same man who appeared on the balcony of St. Peter's and gave the closing address in the Sistine Chapel. Out of the Holy Office (a job he did not like, according to an old friend, as reported in the *New York Times*) he may have much more freedom to be himself. He is certainly well aware of the needs of the American Church in dealing with the pedophile crisis. He has begun a new investigation of Father Maciel. He is reported to have prepared a document that would permit divorced and remarried Catholics to receive the sacraments — though this report has been denied. His enthusiastic right-wing supporters will be horrified if such a document exists.

His German Platonic theological method worries me, but only perhaps because German theologians worry me. Moreover, the rhetoric of his decisions in the Holy Office worry me and worry many people. Obiter dicta such as "gays are fundamentally disordered" and "no one has the right to have a child" are not helpful. The efforts of American cardinals to spin him as a "nice man" (not *spin* but *squirm*, a reporter whispered to me) are a little less than convincing, though he is certainly a nice man. Yet his collegial style as Cardinal Dean is encouraging.

The *London Tablet* tells us that his health is not strong. He is subject to dizzy spells, and this has caused his doctors to beg him not to embark on long airplane flights. Inner ear problems? Presumably he is on strong blood pressure medicine. Presumably also he takes it every day, unlike poor John Paul I, who took his powerful and dangerous medicine erratically.

The *Tablet* also reports that he is liked by cats, who, sensing his affection for them, follow him down the streets of Rome. It also reports that two such favorite cats have been translated to the Vatican Palace, which might help to humanize that cold and impersonal old place.

In his column in the archdiocesan paper, Archbishop Timothy Dolan of Milwaukee tells a story about the new Pope that is worth repeating:

May 25, 2004. Thirty bishops from the American heartland of Wisconsin, Illinois, and Indiana were in Rome for their *ad limina* visit, required of bishops every five years to render an account of their office to the Pope and heads of Vatican congregations. Bishop Richard Sklba and I are among them, and we are ushered into the imposing chambers of the renowned Congregation for the Doctrine of the Faith.

Right on the dot, good German that he is, in walks the prefect, the formidable Cardinal Joseph Ratzinger. Good professor that he is, he begins by telling us what points he wants to consider: the controversy involving some American bishops and politicians, pro-life issues, the sexual abuse scandal, Catholic hospitals, and Catholic universities.

We nod in agreement and sit back and wait for him to begin his "lecture." But instead, he sits back and says, "I need you to help me understand your thoughts and challenges on these issues. Please talk to me."

And did we ever! We probed, questioned, debated, even criticized. An hour and a half later, having himself said little, except for a few perceptive comments and incisive questions, he wraps it up: "Thank you, brothers. You have helped me understand America better. I have so much to learn."

When I served, disastrously if I may say so, on the board of the international journal *Concilium,* I encountered many German theologians. They decided early that I was a "positivist" and, having attached a label, ignored me. I ought not to have been surprised: I was indeed a positivist. I approached reality empirically — I wanted to know what was going on. They approached it "idealistically" — they already knew what was going on (a style from which many American theologians are not immune). As I have written earlier in this book, some of Pope Benedict's comments about "relativism" and "feminism," for example, were of the same sort.

Yet I have to say that not a single of the German theologians on whose windmills I broke my lance ever acted as collegially as Cardinal Ratzinger did in that interview with midwestern bishops or as, according to the American cardinals, he did in the General Congregations. Not a single one admitted that maybe an American empiricist had anything useful to say. Or acted as collegially as my fictional Cardinal Ratzinger did in his conversation with Laurence O'Toole McAuliffe in my story from 1991. It is too early to tell what kind of Pope he will be. We must all give him the benefit of the doubt.

The Pope is not the Church, though some conservative Catholics worship him like he is the Church. Moreover, as successor to Peter, the Pope can be expected to make mistakes, some serious, others not so serious. Like Peter, the Pope is human. He is not God and his powers of infallibility are limited. We perhaps take the Pope too seriously and the long-term impact of the Holy Spirit not seriously enough. The end of the civil rule of the papacy, bitterly denounced by many Popes, freed the Church from enormous burdens and seems clearly the intent of the Spirit.

If you want changes that you think are critical (and may well be critical) by the end of business tomorrow, you will have trouble understanding how slowly human institutions change.

By the next conclave the Church must face the problem of Latin America. I suspect many of the cardinals who did not vote for Benedict XVI are third-world cardinals who are upset that their candidates never had a chance. This conclave was about "stability and continuity." The next one — and I wish Pope Benedict a long and happy life — will be about the third world.

The Church must find a way to deal with papal retirement and/or incapacity that does not force it to choose among candidates who are elderly and perhaps sick. Unlike the LDS we are not a gerontocracy. I do not want to discriminate against elderly candidates — Pope John was only a year younger than Cardinals Martini and Ratzinger when he was elected. There has to be a better way, however, to curtail the length of papal service or to cope with the serious illness of a Pope — even if he is forty-five.

Church leaders must learn to listen, not only because it is sound Catholic doctrine that the Spirit speaks at every level of the Church and the leaders' task is to discern the Spirit but also because if they do not listen, they and the followers will be passing one another like silent ships in the night.

Finally, I can't stress enough the fact that the reevangelization of Europe will be a long task. Pope Benedict and his colleagues should not even begin it until they are committed to listening sympathetically and sensitively. They must also be committed to facing the hard truth that their own actions (or those of their predecessors) may be in part, perhaps in great part, responsible for the alienation of so many men and women in Europe and in the rest of the world.

Though I still love the Church as much as ever and am as angry at it as ever, I won't be at the next conclave should I still be alive at that time. Well, I don't think I will, unless my energy comes back, which doesn't seem likely.* I wonder where Benedict gets his energy. He walks slowly, even more slowly than I do after a lecture.

Despite all the frustrations and hypocrisy, conclaves are addictive. I was happy to escape from Rome. Happy that I didn't have to open my shutters every morning and see the dome of St. Peter's staring at me — a structure for which the Church paid by losing most of North Germany and Scandinavia. That's the way it has been with Rome during my life — delighted to be there, delighted to be out of there.

---

*Please note how the cagey Irishman hedges his bets!

Appendix A

"Hypersexualized" Americans and the
Second and Third Worlds

The International Social Survey Program is now a consortium of nearly forty survey centers that carry out annual studies on commonly determined subjects with commonly drafted questionnaires. In 1998 the subject was religion.

The study found that 18 percent of American Catholics believe premarital sex is always wrong, hardly supporting Vatican spokesman Dr. Navarro-Valls's accusation of "hypersexuality" in America. Of the thirty-two countries surveyed, only the Philippines (61 percent), Brazil (44 percent), Chile and Ireland (29 percent each), Hungary (20 percent), and Slovakia (19 percent) have higher rates of opposition to premarital sex.

In Poland, which surely represents the second world, only 16 percent consider premarital sex to be always wrong. Is Dr. Navarro-Valls ready to denounce Poland as a "hypersexual" country? While Chile, Brazil, and the Philippines represent the third world, only in the latter do a majority of the Catholics disapprove of premarital sex.

Catholics in the United States are more sympathetic to gay sex than are Catholics in most of the countries surveyed, though less so than are German, British, Austrian, Dutch, Czech, Slovene, Canadian, and French Catholics.

One concludes that in the International Social Survey Program's 1998 study, the decline in acceptance of the Catholic sexual ethic recorded in the United States is reflected in most countries, though not on the subject of homosexual sex. The United States hardly appears as a sex-mad country. There is little evidence that the second world presents a brighter future for the Catholic Church, nor does the third world, as far as Brazil and Chile are concerned.

Finally, 54 percent of American Catholics are convinced that abortion is always wrong, behind the Philippines, Brazil, Chile, and Ireland but ahead of the 46 percent in Poland and 30 percent in Slovakia. The notion that Eastern Europe is more virtuous than the United States does not stand up to these data.

Appendix B

What the Laity Want in a Pope — A Study in Six Countries*

To separate Catholics' ideal image of the Church from their personal loyalty (or animus) to the present Pope, we asked them about the next Pope — the one who would be chosen by the cardinals after the death or retirement of Pope John Paul II. We introduced the questions this way:

> We are interested in what type of leader Catholics would like to see elected the next Pope. As you may know, when a Pope dies the cardinals meet in Rome to elect the next Pope. The last time a Pope was elected was in 1978, when Pope John Paul II was elected.

We followed this preamble with seven questions (more in some countries) that addressed concerns with the institutional form of the Catholic Church. We did not ask about doctrinal issues — save arguably the ordination of women — or matters of faith:

*Italy, Poland, Germany, Spain, Ireland, United States

1. Which would you consider more important in choosing a Pope, that the Pope show more concern about what life is like for ordinary people or that the Pope show more concern about religious issues?

2. Would you favor or oppose the next Pope permitting priests to marry?

3. Currently Catholic bishops are appointed by the Vatican. In the past bishops were elected by priests and people within their own dioceses. Would you prefer the next Pope to continue to appoint bishops or would you prefer to have bishops chosen by priests and people within their own diocese?

4. How would you feel about letting representative laypeople have more of a voice in the Catholic Church, for example by serving as advisers to the Pope? Would you favor this?

5. Would you like to see the next Pope give more decision-making power to the bishops in this country or do you think the Pope should continue to make most of the decisions for the Church?

6. Would you favor or oppose the next Pope allowing the ordination of women to the priesthood?

7. Would you like the next Pope to be more open to change in the Church or do you think things are okay the way they are?

A majority of the laity support change of some sort in each country, and in some countries, majorities support all seven reforms we proposed to them.

The most reform-minded countries are Spain, Germany, and Ireland. Catholics in these three countries want change more than any of the others. Each of the seven reforms gets support from more than 58 percent of Catholics in all three countries. The average support for each question is 78 percent in Germany, 74 percent in Spain, and 73 percent in Ireland. The exact profile of support differs slightly between them. The Spanish Catholics give particularly strong support to the proposition that the Pope should attend to the life of the laity and grant their bishops more autonomy; they are less keen about the election of local bishops. The Irish Catholics and German Catholics particularly favor lay advisers and married priests. Support for the ordination of women is highest in these two countries as well.

The United States and Italy fall in the middle of the six countries in this study. American Catholics endorse six of the seven items by roughly a two-to-one margin. The exception is the item about autonomy for local bishops, which gets "only" 58-percent support. The Italians are among the most populist nations, with 77 percent supporting a Pope who will emphasize the life of the laity over religious themes. On the other hand, autonomy for local bishops fails (by two percentage points) to get a majority. The Italians also show a lower level of support for "a Pope open to change" than would be expected from their support for specific changes.

Polish Catholics, on the other hand, support specific reforms less than might be expected given their strong (58 percent) support for a Pope more open to change. A majority of Poles support the election of bishops, autonomy for bishops, an emphasis on the life of the laity, and marriage for priests. The call for lay advisers falls one percentage point short of a majority. Only ordination of women is strongly opposed — but that by a three-to-one margin. This issue drives the Polish average for change just under half.

Remarkably, the only reform to win a majority of support in all six countries is the election of bishops. Remarkable, because this issue is not an item on any group's agenda for change. Many respondents were probably stating an opinion on the matter for the first time when they answered this question (unlike some other issues, such as the ordination of women and allowing priests to marry, which are widely discussed). They answered in a manner consistent with the democratic institutions that surround them. Each of the six countries selects its head of government and local officials democratically. When asked about selecting a Church leader democratically, they responded in the affirmative.

Could it be that some Catholics seek reform in some issue domains, say church governance, while others emphasize their issues, say ordination of women, without much general support for change? It could be, but it is not that way. The support for reform lies along a clear proreform/antireform continuum in each country. We performed factor analyses of the seven items in each country and found a single dominant factor in each.

Catholics under forty and those with an academic education more strongly support reform than do older and less-educated Catholics. We can see this by comparing responses to the election of bishops. (Similar patterns hold for the other six items, so going through all the results would be redundant.)

The younger Catholics in each country support election of bishops more than do older ones. Seventy-one percent of the

Irish under forty support the election of bishops, compared with 68 percent of Americans, 62 percent of Spaniards, 61 percent of Poles, and 60 percent of Italians.

Academically educated Catholics in each country support the election of bishops more than do less-educated Catholics. Seventy percent of Irish with an academic secondary education, some university education, or a degree from a university support the election of bishops, compared with 66 percent of similarly educated Spaniards, 65 percent of Americans with some college experience or a degree, 61 percent of Poles with academic secondary or university education, and 60 percent of Italians with that kind of education.

American women give more support to reform than do American men on every issue *except* the ordination of women — an issue on which, interestingly enough, *men* are more supportive. Gender gaps are much less pervasive elsewhere. In Spain, Ireland, and Poland, men and women do not differ significantly on the election of bishops or most other items. In Italy, however, 64 percent of men but only 46 percent of women support election of bishops.

It is worth repeating that only the ordination of women is a doctrinal issue on which a "definitive" decision was made by Pope John Paul. All the other issues are disciplinary or customary and could be changed tomorrow.

Appendix C

Can the Church Change?

Judge John Noonan* answers that question at considerable length in his recent book *A Church That Can and Cannot Change* (University of Notre Dame Press, 2005). In his previous book *Contraception,* he pointed out that there has been a change in the Church's attitude toward contraception since the nineteenth century. When the French began to cope with their population explosion by the use of coitus interruptus, the French bishops asked the Holy Office how they should deal with the problem. The first response instructed them to proceed cautiously. The second adjured them not to trouble the conscience of the faithful, a stand taken by Saint Jean Vianney, the famous Cure d'Ars, in his conferences for confessors. The point is not that the doctrine has changed but that at one time the Church did not want to trouble the consciences of the faithful. Unfortunately, since 1930 it has done its best to do exactly that, with, according to the data, very little impact since 1968.

*Philosopher, historian, lawyer, professor at the University of Notre Dame and the University of California at Berkeley, and federal judge of the Ninth Appellate Court.

However, in the new book Judge Noonan discusses three previous changes that I now propose for those people who say the Church can't change — slavery, religious freedom, and the indissolubility of marriage. He observes that all three of these changes involve matters that were said to be intrinsic to the natural law.

From the beginning of Christianity until the late nineteenth century the Church argued that slavery was in keeping with the natural law. Such a position was taught by almost every Pope and almost every theologian (save for the theologian Cajetan) who addressed the question, including Cardinal Newman. Priests, religious orders, and nuns owned slaves — and often pursued them when they ran away. At the end of the nineteenth century, Pope Leo XIII was the first to express disapproval. Only at the Second Vatican Council did the Church formally condemn slavery and only in John Paul II's encyclical *Veritatis Splendor* was it finally said after two millennia of outrageous injustice that slavery was intrinsically evil. From "in keeping with the natural law" to "intrinsically evil" in a hundred fifty years: for the Catholic Church that's quick change.

For most of its history the Church also approved the use of force to suppress error. In the middle of the nineteenth century Popes wrote documents saying that it was evil to suggest that error had any rights. Fifty years ago Jesuit John Courtney Murray was silenced for writing about religious freedom, an entirely new and dangerous idea, it seemed. Yet Father Murray, God be good to him, wrote the basic draft of religious freedom at the Second Vatican Council that was adopted as the document *Dignitatis Humanae* by a vote of 2,308 to 70. In the space of fifteen years John Murray had made the pilgrimage from a silenced Jesuit to a concelebrant of the final Mass of the council with the Pope. That was a very quick change, a reversal of at least fifteen hundred years of history. Indeed, the change was quicker than that. Father Murray was "disinvited" to the first session of the council, and at the fourth session he was a hero. In its insight into the truth that the act of faith must be free, *Of Human Dignity* may be the most important document of the council.

Despite a long history of insisting that divorce is against the natural law, the Church has also a long history of dissolving some marriages under certain conditions. In the twentieth century it modified its position to claim to have power to dissolve all marriages between two people who were not baptized and even marriages in which one member was not baptized — which as Judge Noonan observes is claiming jurisdiction over five-sixths of the human race. Moreover new norms were developed for "annulments," which declared that for one reason or another some marriages had not been valid from the beginning. Finally, many priests are invoking an "internal forum solution." This is a situation in which a couple believes a prior marriage was not valid, but they cannnot, for one reason or another, bring the union to question before an ecclesiastical court to seek an annulment. They may decide for themselves, presumably with the advice of a priest, whether they are free to marry and contract marriage by an exchange of promises, though there is no church marriage. Some priests say a Mass for them and bless them. As a highly reputable pastor puts it, "There is no marriage problem that we can't resolve in a rectory office."

The Church at various levels is obviously groping toward a different approach to marriage. The German bishops have repeatedly asked that the divorced and remarried might receive the sacraments. Rumors in Rome suggest that the new Pope is not totally averse to such a solution, though the rumors are denied and one may be skeptical about their likelihood under Pope Benedict.

Such a permission would shut down the annulment mills in American chanceries and the internal forum decisions in the rectories, thus solving in practice a question that is still difficult in theory.

I am not a theologian or a prophet, so I hazard no guesses about further changes in the Church. Judge Noonan points out that the Church often changes without admitting that it has changed. He also suggests that what happens in the change is that the Church grows in its understanding of human nature. Thus after centuries the Church finally came to understand that it was against human nature — intrinsically evil — that one human should own another and that one human's act of faith be forced by another. The Church does not and should not change to keep up with the times. But it can change and should change as its knowledge of human nature grows richer, more complex, and deeper. That has happened at least four times since the American Civil War and indeed twice since 1960 — the later changes being critical issues of human freedom: freedom from slavery and freedom of religious faith.

The next big change? Without making any predictions about when it will come (perhaps later than sooner) or what it will lead to, I do believe there will be a gradual discovery of the fundamental equality of women — "neither male nor female, but all one in Christ Jesus." One hopes only that the Church will not be the last to discover that reality.

About the Author

A native of Chicago, Father Andrew M. Greeley is a priest, distinguished sociologist, and bestselling author. He is a professor of social sciences at the University of Arizona, as well as a research associate at the National Opinion Research Center at the University of Chicago, and he does weekend parish work in both Chicago and Tucson. He writes a weekly syndicated column for the *Chicago Sun-Times* and has funded a chair in Catholic studies at the University of Chicago.